Instead of pretending to be something we're not, Jonathan Murphy invites us to become what we are. Barnabas points the way as a man in Christ, like Christ, who lived for Christ. Good stuff. Biblical, practical, and really helpful. It helped me.

ALISTAIR BEGG, PARKSIDE CHURCH, CHAGRIN FALLS, OHIO

I know Jonathan Murphy to be a truly authentic pastor, leader, and follower of Jesus. *Authentic Influencer* is his study and insight into Barnabas, which could almost be autobiographical! I've had the blessing of walking with Jonathan as this resource has come to fruition, and I'm excited for every believer to read it! It will not only encourage you, but it will inspire you to make a difference for Jesus.

TODD LANE, EXECUTIVE SENIOR PASTOR, GATEWAY CHURCH

God loves people. Every person was made for God and is worth influencing for Him. There is no higher calling than to shape a life for Christ. And we all get to do it! But *how*? Jonathan Murphy's book *Authentic Influencer* helps us with the *why* and *how*. Every believer who wants to make a difference in another life for Christ will benefit from this book.

CHIP DICKENS, PhD, DEPARTMENT CHAIR AND
ENDOWED PROFESSOR OF COUNSELING MINISTRIES
AT DALLAS THEOLOGICAL SEMINARY

When an author writes a book about authentic Christian leadership, you want to be sure the writer is practicing what he's preaching. In the case of *Authentic Influencer*, I can tell you firsthand that this is a book written by a genuinely humble and authentic Christian leader. His new book is simple and insightful, engaging and inspiring, as well as biblical and practical. If you live out the principles modeled from the life of Barnabas in this book, then your marriage, family, friendships, and neighborhoods will be impacted for Jesus Christ.

BRENT EVANS, CEO OF XO MARRIAGE

Barnabas is a saint who has too long lived in the shadow of other New Testament giants. Dr. Murphy brings this overlooked servant into the light to illuminate a humble example all of us need to emulate today.

DR. CODY MCQUEEN, LEAD PASTOR, CHRIST
CHAPEL BIBLE CHURCH, FORT WORTH, TEXAS

What a guy, that Barnabas! Everybody needs one. And Jonathan Murphy will be yours, via the printed word. You know why? Because everybody needs to be a Barnabas too, and Dr. Murphy will nudge you in the direction to becoming one yourself. That's how nobodies like you and me become somebodies for everybody! And thus the church of God is made fully functional, all body parts optimally working as they ought to, building one another in love, until we all become like Christ for the glory of God. So take and read. Then go and encourage.

DR. ABRAHAM KURUVILLA, CARL E. BATES
PROFESSOR OF CHRISTIAN PREACHING, THE
SOUTHERN BAPTIST THEOLOGICAL SEMINARY

It's been said that "influence is the exhalation of character." Jonathan Murphy embodies that truth. He has been a consistent, faithful, encouraging influencer in my life and ministry for many years. I trust his wisdom and value his counsel. We all have influence for good or for bad. If you want to maximize your influence for good and for God, read this book. Those around you will be glad you did.

DR. MARK HITCHCOCK, SENIOR PASTOR, FAITH BIBLE
CHURCH, EDMOND, OK; RESEARCH PROFESSOR OF BIBLE
EXPOSITION, DALLAS THEOLOGICAL SEMINARY

We all want to know how we can impact our culture for Christ. With the current loss of respect for Christian truth in the public square, it seems most of us have become somewhat hesitant to boldly live out our faith. Jonathan Murphy draws on a lesser-known character in

Scripture as a timeless guide. Through the life of Barnabas and with engaging illustrations, Dr. Murphy skillfully leads us through this great encourager's life as a model that all can follow. With wisdom and wit, *Authentic Influencer* is the catalyst we need to live out our faith in a society desperately needing to see Jesus.

RHOME VAN DYCK, PRESIDENT, SACRA SCRIPT MINISTRIES

Some people are basement people, and some people are balcony people. Basement people are those who bring you down and siphon you of life. Balcony people are those who lift you up and cheer you on. In this wonderful book Jonathan Murphy introduces us to the consummate balcony person, Barnabas, Mr. Encourager himself. Read these insights on the life of an "authentic influencer" and be inspired to encourage and influence those around you toward and for Christ. C. H. Spurgeon said to "carve not your name on marble but on hearts." Study the life of Barnabas with Jonathan and start etching godliness on others.

PHILIP DE COURCY, PASTOR OF KINDRED COMMUNITY CHURCH, ANAHEIM HILLS, CALIFORNIA, AND TEACHER ON THE DAILY RADIO PROGRAM *KNOW THE TRUTH*

I believe that in the heart of every young believer is a deep desire to live a life of influence. We are here to be salt and light in a dark and broken world, but the question is how do we do that? Dr. Murphy uses the ordinary yet incredibly inspiring life of Barnabas as a helpful compass for us to look to and learn from as we seek to make our lives count for God's glory. Every young leader should read this book!

GRANT PARTRICK, PASSION CITY CHURCH ATLANTA

AUTHENTIC INFLUENCER

THE BARNABAS WAY OF
SHAPING LIVES FOR JESUS

AUTHENTIC
INFLUENCER

JONATHAN MURPHY

W PUBLISHING GROUP

AN IMPRINT OF THOMAS NELSON

Published in Nashville, Tennessee, by W Publishing, an imprint of Thomas Nelson.

Published in association with the literary agency Yates & Yates.

Thomas Nelson titles may be purchased in bulk for educational, business, fundraising, or sales promotional use. For information, please email SpecialMarkets@ThomasNelson.com.

Any internet addresses, phone numbers, or company or product information printed in this book are offered as a resource and are not intended in any way to be or to imply an endorsement by Thomas Nelson, nor does Thomas Nelson vouch for the existence, content, or services of these sites, phone numbers, companies, or products beyond the life of this book.

ISBN 978-1-4003-3334-2(audiobook)
ISBN 978-1-4003-3331-8(eBook)
ISBN 978-1-4003-3330-1 (softcover)

Library of Congress Control Number

2022950360

Printed in the United States of America
22 23 24 25 26 LBC 5 4 3 2 1

To Dad.
My Barnabas.

Contents

CONTENTS

Foreword

GENERATION Z LIVES BY THE RECOMMENDATIONS OF so-called "social media influencers" who share their choice of sunglasses, sneakers, beverages, and more. Some of those influencers make huge impacts on their followers when it comes to product endorsements while making seven-figure incomes just telling people what face cream to use. Sounds absurd, doesn't it? But it's reality, especially among the younger generations.

Imagine if more Christians were intentional in trying to be influencers for the Master instead of for money or for more followers and likes? Young and creative believers have an incredible opportunity to influence their generation for an eternity with Jesus instead of for their next purchases. In fact, whether you are young or old or somewhere in between, there are opportunities all around for you to influence others for Jesus.

That kind of legacy influencing is the vision of Dr. Jonathan Murphy, a new and younger voice in the evangelical Christian world, who was influenced himself to write this book by the person who could easily be nominated as the most influential person in the Bible, other than Jesus Himself.

Most Christians know of Barnabas only as a drive-by encourager in the New Testament church who is occasionally mentioned in the book of Acts and the letters of the apostle Paul. Why was he so influential in the New Testament, and how does he have such great relevance for us today? First, he was divinely chosen to be the role model of the type of influencer God wants us all to be. And second, God wants us to know that even today influencers like Barnabas can produce world changers like Paul. Together, we all can make an impact in this world, for the glory of God.

Dr. Murphy has carefully investigated the life and influence of Barnabas. In *Authentic Influencer*, he shares insights for everyday believers—grassroots, accessible, and godly ways—on how to influence our culture for Jesus. The principles presented in this book are rooted in the Scriptures. And their practicality will inspire and instruct you so that you know how to move from being a spectator of God's work to actively participating in what He is doing in the world and in what He wants to do in *and* through you.

As Dr. Murphy mentions in this book, Barnabas *shows* us rather than *tells* us how to influence the world for Jesus Christ. Barnabas is a natural template for everyday believers—from pastors and ministry leaders to corporate CEOs to stay-at-home parents and more.

Dr. Murphy's vision also includes an understanding that all of us as part of the body of Christ must use our influence to shape the world for Jesus. That's a godly vision! *Authentic Influencer* will help us leave an everlasting and indelible imprint on this generation and those to come.

—Governor Mike Huckabee

Introduction

Go and make disciples . . .
JESUS

Remember who you are and
Whom you serve.
W. D. MURPHY

MY DAD SHAPED MY LIFE. DAD DOES THAT. HE INFLU-
ences people. It's all very natural to him. Ask anyone who
knows him, and you'll find they all agree: if you are within
earshot of Pastor Murphy long enough, he *will* impact your
life. Often, it's subtle with a joke here or an encouraging word
there. At times it's more direct through a piece of godly advice,
a timely prayer, or a Bible verse that whispers God's voice when
you need to hear it most. Either way, subtle or not, Dad impacts
and inspires people. And he's contagious. You want to be like
the guy! Dad has a knack for impacting *all* who draw near.

A priceless picture is etched in my mind from years of daily
exposure. Recalling it always puts a smile on my face and moti-
vates me to walk well with God. Now, that's a powerful image!
Every morning as a kid, I arose and headed to the kitchen for
breakfast. In order to get there, I passed through our living
room, which is where I'd first see Dad. He was unmissable. His
glasses were placed on an open Bible on the chair beside him.
His face was cradled in the palms of his hands. And he was
on his knees in prayer chatting with God. It was as if Dad had
become part of the room's furniture every night. Long before
dawn, Dad was up meeting with God.

That scene—a memory that I hope never fades—was
repeated throughout the day in different places. If you walked

into Dad's run-down office in the basement of the church, you'd see the same thing: a few sermon notes scribbled on a notepad beside his Bible, glasses off, and Dad on his knees, face in hands in prayer. When he took us to school in the morning, the radio was always kept off, a Bible verse was always shared, a song was always sung, and prayers were always raised. Car rides were prime time to shape his children for Christ just before we stepped into the big, bad world. And as we climbed out of the car and wandered into school to start our day, his parting words were ringing in our ears: "Kids, remember who you are and Whom you serve."

Those daily words and visual pictures molded my life. They still do. Ongoing exposure to scenes like that—an authentic man of God living devoted to Him—shapes and sculpts those who draw near. "Who is Dad's God?" I'd often ask. "How awesome must *He* be, given my dad is devoted to Him?" That type of natural and authentic Christian living grabs you and shapes you. It drew me to want to know Dad's God too. Authentic Christians like Dad just living out their ordinary lives for Christ *can* change the world around them one person at a time by God's design!

You, too, have been shaped by people and events around you. If you pause for a moment and reflect on it, memories will surface of people who impacted your life in specific ways. It's because God made each one of us moldable. It's as simple as that. Human beings are easily shaped. You may not like to hear this, but the truth is you are as malleable as Play-Doh in the hands of a child. It's true. We all are like putty in the hands of those forces of influence around us, especially our immediate culture.

Take just one tiny example: our taste buds. I'm convinced no human being naturally likes the taste of black coffee. At least not initially. Yet many of us yearn for it every morning—it's become a necessity. Through exposure day in and day out, our taste buds are conditioned to like coffee (perhaps initially just to stay awake). But repeated exposure trains—no, converts!—your taste buds to become passionate about coffee. And the data shows how profitable our malleable taste buds are for the coffee market. In the United States consumers spent $74.2 billion on coffee recently, the industry is responsible for 1,694,710 jobs, and it generates around $28 billion in taxes.[1] And let's not talk about our conditioning toward sugar!

The fact that we are shaped by what is around us isn't surprising if you think about it scripturally. It simply comes down to our basic human makeup. We are made of clay, and clay is moldable. The Bible teaches that God, like a potter, formed us from the dust of the earth.[2] Therefore, it makes sense that our taste buds, our speech, our accents, our mannerisms, hobbies, outlooks, opinions, pursuits, passions—the desires of our hearts—are all easily shaped by those influences around us.

And what is perhaps the most powerful earthly influence on a human being *by God's design*? Another human being! Of all the outside influences that form us, other people shape us most. While the teaching is clear throughout the Scriptures, Proverbs 13:20 says it nicely in one spot: "Whoever walks with the wise becomes wise, but the companion of fools will suffer harm" (ESV). One of God's major instruments to shape a life is another life.

The issue is not just whether we are impressionable and malleable. That's a settled matter. The question is, *Who* shapes us? According to whose template are you continually molded— bit by bit, day in and day out? Moreover, who do *you* shape? What influence spreads from you? Dad was a template for me: a natural and godly template. I didn't know I was being shaped every morning, and Dad wasn't always aware of his formative influence either. This was just regular life; it was authentic Christian living. But think about it for a few seconds longer; there is a reason why kids not only sound like their mom or dad but act like them too. It's because all people are like natural environments that others enter when they come close; we are all microcosms that impact those who draw near. Just being exposed to Dad's authentic passion for Jesus daily grew a nat- ural desire in me to authentically want to know and follow Jesus. An authentic life influences others. And I've a sneaking suspicion he's the reason I need a morning coffee!

Just like my dad, we all are a portable environment everywhere we go. And just as Dad influenced me with a mini- culture that oozed authentic and contagious zeal for God, we have the opportunity to naturally influence those around us for Christ. That is precisely God's call on every believer. *Every* believer. In our routine comings and goings as followers *of* Jesus, God wants us to naturally influence those around us *for* Jesus. That's the Great Commission. That's how God chooses to work.

Let's pause for a moment over Jesus' parting words in the Great Commission of Matthew 28:19–20. His call is that Christians would "go and make disciples." It is a call to followers of Jesus to actively pursue (go) influence for Christ over others around them (make disciples) so that these others will also become followers of Jesus (and go and make disciples too). All this while going about regular, everyday life wherever that takes place and with whoever happens to be right there beside you—quietly or loudly, publicly or anonymously. Pastors and parishioners alike, the call goes to all.

It is God's will that *every* Christian exert influence on others for Jesus Christ—to shape the lives of others to one extent or another. You don't get to subcontract the Great Commission to your pastor. You don't get to hide in the pews as you wait for heaven. You don't get to spectate on Christ's work in the world from the sidelines. And, of course, you don't need to be in a position or office of influence with some sort of fancy leadership title to obey this primary command. You can obey it from the very spot God put you in and for the benefit of whoever happens to be close by.

This is the way it once was. Christianity spread at a tremendous pace in the first few centuries of the Christian era (despite massive obstacles) precisely because *every* believer saw it as his or her devotion and duty to influence whoever happened to be near them in life.[3] Christians back then were on the edges of society. They were not considered important. They were deemed weird and insignificant and killjoys. But from that very spot on the edges of influence, ordinary believers were daily making disciples.

Everyday Christian women, men, children, business owners, stay-at-home parents, butchers, bakers, and candlestick makers (just ordinary Christians living out their faith authentically) changed their little sphere of life for Jesus Christ. They, too, had insecurities, fears of rejection, and limited Bible knowledge. Most didn't preach sermons from pulpits. Most didn't write books. But most *did* understand the Great Commission as a beautiful act of devotion and personal responsibility to Jesus Christ. They knew they—not their pastor on their behalf—would stand before Jesus one day and render an account for those people near them in daily life.[4] Consequently, everyday believers lived for Jesus faithfully by loving others practically.

The result? Within a few centuries, the pagan culture that crucified Jesus and pushed Christians around ended up on bended knee proclaiming that "Jesus Christ is Lord."[5] Remember, this happened at growth rates yet to be matched! That could happen again. The question is how.

God provided a practical and accessible way for believers to naturally influence their slice of the world for Jesus Christ. God does not give us a definition of an authentic life of influence, but He gave us an example of someone who modeled it. His name is Barnabas.

Barnabas lived out a faith that we can copy. He pops in and out of the book of Acts but is never central in any scene. You would just read right past him (and probably have on many occasions!), not really noticing the significance of his life. That's because Barnabas was just an ordinary Christian; he was an everyday member of a local church. He was no big shot. Barnabas was no apostle Paul. He did not write multiple letters that would become part of the Scriptures. Barnabas never wrote a gospel on the life of Christ. We don't have any sermon he ever preached. Barnabas was no walking-on-water apostle Peter, holding the keys to the kingdom. Barnabas was just an ordinary farmer from the island of Cyprus who was part parishioner, part pastor, part missionary, and even part mailman!

But Barnabas, as you will see, was always alert to God's workings in his surroundings; he was sensitive to the voice of God. And Barnabas was always available to do what God needed done; he didn't care if the matter was big or small. Barnabas was always a breath of fresh air to those around him: he encouraged the apostles, he encouraged Paul, and he encouraged the churches in Jerusalem, Antioch, and all over what is modern-day Turkey. No, Barnabas didn't write any book on theology or an epistle in the Bible, but he did give us the apostle Paul. He didn't write a gospel, but he gave us John Mark, the author of the Gospel of Mark. It is also believed that under Barnabas's ministry in Antioch, Dr. Luke—the author of the Gospel of Luke and the Acts of the Apostles— came to faith. Yes, Barnabas was just an everyday Christian, but he is a perfect example of how God uses ordinary believers to accomplish His extraordinary purposes on earth.

From the story of Barnabas, we can see fifteen principles

on how everyday Christians like us can develop an authentic life of influence too—a life that shapes the culture for God. Over the years I've observed in my own life as a pastor and professor that my most meaningful influence has been in those everyday spheres of life rather than at Sunday morning pulpits or seminary lecterns. While these are important, it's been the everyday conversations with a neighbor, with a student after class, or during time spent over coffee with a friend that have had the most influence. And that is the way God works every day through everyday believers. It is in the regular and routine areas of life that natural relationships are found and lasting influence occurs. These fifteen principles from the life of Barnabas help you there. They are not a step-by-step method on how to lead others formally; they are principles to adapt and customize so that everyday believers like us can learn how to influence others in regular life *Christ's* way—be it one person at a time or a group.

I know what you are thinking. You have flaws, fears, limitations, perhaps a poor track record so far, or you simply don't think you have the "right" personality. And I know that others around you seem so talented and capable. God wants to use them. Just them, right? Wrong! God has a knack for using the unlikely who live in the ordinary ebb and flow of life to change neighborhoods for Him.

Remember the first twelve followers? Pastor Gene Getz makes my point for me with a little humor. Allow me to pass it on. It's a funny and fictional email from a recruitment agency giving a final recommendation to its client on personnel selections for a global project. The client is Jesus.

> Thank you for submitting the résumés of the twelve men you have picked for management positions in your new organization. All of them have now taken our battery of tests; and we have not only run the results through our computer, but also arranged personal interviews for each of them with our psychologist and vocational aptitude consultant.
>
> It is the staff's opinion that most of your nominees are lacking in background, education, and vocational aptitude for the type of enterprise you are undertaking.
>
> Simon Peter is emotionally unstable and given to fits of temper. Andrew has no qualities of leadership. The two brothers, James and John, sons of Zebedee, place personal interests above company loyalty. Thomas demonstrates a questioning attitude that would tend to undermine morale. We feel it our duty to tell you that Matthew has been blacklisted by the Greater Jerusalem Better Business Bureau. James, the son of Alphaeus, and particularly Simon the Zealot have radical leanings, and they both registered a high score on the manic-depressive scale. Thaddaeus is definitely sensitive, but he wants to make everyone happy.
>
> One of the candidates, however, shows great potential. He is a man of ability and resourcefulness, meets people well, has a keen business mind, and has contacts in high places. He is highly motivated, ambitious, and responsible.

We recommend Judas Iscariot as your controller and right-hand man. All of the other profiles are self-explanatory. We wish you every success in your new venture.[6]

Jesus wants to use ordinary believers to shape their part of the world for Him. But these become authentic Christian disciples by the influence of others who stepped up for Christ along the way too. That must be you—flaws and all!

Some Food for Thought

BEFORE ANSWERING THE FOLLOWING QUESTIONS either in personal study or as part of a group, revisit the teaching in this chapter and think it through.

1. Humans are malleable. We are made of clay. Spend some time reflecting on how you became the person you are today. Make a list of the influences, both positive and negative (and both subtle or direct), that form human hearts (including yours).

2. If you are a follower *of* Jesus Christ, you are a follower *for* Jesus Christ. The Great Commission is that you would "go and make disciples." Read Matthew 28:19–20. Note the implications of this for your life. What are some natural everyday relationships where you could start?

3. Form an authentic servant leader and the church gets godly servant leadership. What is essential to the formation of an authentic leader for ministry?

CHAPTER 1

Influencers

Flavoring Society for Jesus

You are the salt of the earth.
You are the light of the world.
JESUS

Genuine leadership is measured by influence—
nothing more, nothing less.
JOHN C. MAXWELL

THE LOUD KNOCK ON OUR FRONT DOOR NEARLY woke the entire Spanish village of Jinámar. It was siesta time. Who messes with the national midday nap? It seems Fernando didn't care. He was on a personal mission and was in town for only a few minutes. When one of us eventually opened the door, Fernando asked, "Is Father Murphy home?"

Jinámar is a place in the Canary Islands that no one wants to visit. Millions of tourists descend on these islands every year, but the location of Jinámar is a well-kept secret by design. For decades it was just another Spanish village: lots of little white houses glistening in the sun built around a public square and huddled up to the chief boss right at the center of town—the Roman Catholic Church. But in the 1970s everything changed. Spain changed. The longtime dictator, Francisco Franco, died, and Spain's most valuable resources went on the global market: sun, sand, and sea.

Millions of northern Europeans—Germans, Brits, Swedes, Dutch—descended on the islands for some year-round fun in the sun. But there was one problem. What about all the poor and unemployed locals who lived in cardboard huts and shacks on those great tourist beaches? What an inconvenience! That would soon bring an economic boom to bust.

The solution was to build the Valley of Jinámar beside

the beautiful Village of Jinámar. It was a government housing plan—a ghetto of sorts—to get those deemed the riffraff of society out of tourist view. Thousands were picked up from the beaches, dropped off in newly built twenty-story buildings, and left to fend for themselves. It was in a valley off the beaten path, so it was out of sight and its new inhabitants would be confined. It was to be a well-kept secret by design: don't let those tourists know! The result of thousands of people living with no money, no jobs, no prospects, little education, and no way out of that vicious cycle was disastrous. Jinámar became the hub of the island's crime, prostitution, drug traffic, and gang warfare.

Well, Jinámar is where God called my parents to serve. For decades the light of the gospel shone in that dark corner of the world as they planted and pastored a little church. They held services, open-air meetings, and Sunday school classes. They handed out gospel tracts, went on house-to-house visitations, visited the local prison, ran summer youth camps and vacation Bible school, and (my favorite) Saturday morning kids' club. I loved it!

Every Saturday morning Dad hopped into his big, old, rusty van and headed into the ghetto to pick up children for kids' club. This was an *old* van. And noisy! In some places you could see the asphalt road through small rust holes on the van floor. It had a loudspeaker fitted on top that played music and let the street kids know it was pickup time. "God is Love" and "God loves you" were spray-painted on all sides. It looked like a Sherman tank, so we called it the Gospel Tank. It was like a

Pied Piper summoning kids in this rough and unwanted corner of the world to share with them the love of Jesus Christ.

"Is Father Murphy home?" Fernando repeated.

Dad wasn't home and wouldn't be back anytime soon. Fernando was disappointed because he couldn't stick around. He was leaving the island immediately with no plans to ever return. He asked if he could leave a message to be passed on to Dad, which went like this:

Would you tell Father Murphy that my name is Fernando? He won't remember me. I'm in my late twenties now. I've spent the last decade on drugs, in crime, and in and out of prisons across Spain. I eventually ended up on my deathbed in a drug rehabilitation center in northern Spain.

I'm in town visiting my mom but I will not be back. But I need Father Murphy to know that I used to come here on Saturday mornings as a little boy. It was the highlight of my week. I got to ride in a big, rusty van with him, sing songs, hear stories, and then get what I wanted most of all, a small cookie and a quarter cup of soda. I was always hungry. I *loved* cookie and Coke time!

Eventually, I stopped coming and got caught up in the life I just described. But here's the thing. As I lay in my prison cells at night for years and as I lay overdosed on drugs many, many times over, all I could hear running through my head were those beautiful songs, those Bible stories and verses, and that message on that big, old, rusty van: "God is Love." "God loves you." He loves *me*? How is that possible?

I want Father Murphy to know that I am now a follower of Jesus Christ. God pursued me all those years watering a seed that Father Murphy planted in my heart. I'm here simply to say thank you. Would you thank Father Murphy for loving the children of Jinámar? He needs to know that he influenced this place and that *God* changed my life.

AUTHENTIC INFLUENCE MATTERS

Influence matters. It happens all around us. It's not a question of whether it occurs but what type is occurring. Some influence is positive. Much of it is negative. At times it is direct, loud, and quick. Other times it is subtle, silent, slow, even barely detected. As we saw in the introduction, we are very malleable, and people often influence us most and set the specific directions of our lives. Sometimes it's just a simple message of God's love on the side of an old, rusty van that plants a seed in a heart. Isn't it wonderful that life-changing influence can occur anywhere and by anyone?

I recently read the story of Duncan Campbell and was impacted by his life. Duncan was an influential preacher in Scotland whom God put in the pulpit to preach the gospel. Thousands bowed the knee to Jesus Christ. His ministry was much like Billy Graham's, albeit in just one specific spot in the world. And while the biography focused on his preaching ministry and the Hebrides Revival, what caught my attention most was his mother's formative and authentic influence on his life.

Jane Campbell was a woman whose entire life didn't extend much beyond a few miles from her home, where she raised lots and lots of kids. But that home was a place of ministry for the kingdom of God. Her home was an altar of worship to God. On the living room rug, at the kitchen table, or seated by the fire on endless cold nights, day after day, Jane shaped little lives for Jesus Christ. These were ordinary household spots, but they rivaled grand cathedrals in their use. They were sacred spaces. At the kitchen table, day in and day out, and surrounded by dirty dishes and sniffly noses, Jane Campbell worshiped God by teaching her children of His love. Jane "lived, and loved, and prayed until in old age, after much suffering, with the Bible still propped up before her and a heavenly light glowing on her face, she fell asleep in Jesus. Duncan never forgot the debt he owed to his mother. How thankful he was that he had a mother who knew God."[1] The Hebrides Revival began decades earlier at an everyday believer's kitchen table; it was the private ministry of a stay-at-home mom long before it blossomed years later as her son's pulpit ministry.

And what about another everyday Scotsman named John Campbell? There is just one line about him in the book I was reading, but it got me digging to learn more about his life. He was not a direct relative of Jane and Duncan, just part of the same Campbell clan. Here was a man keen to serve God in vocational ministry, but ill health put a stop to that. As a result, John ran a post office in the rocky seashore area of Ledaig, Benderloch. There, for fifty years, John taught the Bible, led prayer gatherings, and ran children's Bible clubs. For twenty-three of those years, these worship gatherings took place in a most remarkable spot: a sea cave!

In that cave, under the light of an oil lamp, with a large tree stump as a pulpit (and when the sea tide was out), John proclaimed God. And this was not just any tree stump. King Robert the Bruce of Scotland supposedly used it as a makeshift table many centuries before. What a blessing this cave preacher was to that little society and beyond. Moms and dads brought their kids to learn the Bible from the one who had taught them the same truths in that very cave when they, too, were young. And even those he discipled, who then left and scattered across the earth, did "come back on a visit to the dear old country of their birth, from Australia, New Zealand, Canada, or the States, [and] always find their way to Ledaig, sure to get a cordial welcome and a firm grip of the hand from their much-loved and respected teacher."[2]

Influence really matters. Authentic godly influence can occur *anywhere*: in vans that become gospel tanks, from pulpits that bring spiritual revival, at kitchen tables one-on-one, and even in sea caves. And that influence can occur by *anyone* who is a follower of Jesus Christ: next-to-nobody preachers, next-to-nobody mailmen, next-to-nobody stay-at-home moms, next-to-nobody CEOs, next-to-nobody grannies, next-to-nobody gardeners, and the list goes on.

Lastly but most importantly, godly influence must be *every* Christian's stamp on the world. Well, that's according to Jesus Christ!

THE CALL OF JESUS' FIRST SERMON: BE MY INFLUENCER

Jesus' first sermon—and His most famous one at that—is the Sermon on the Mount (found in Matthew 5–7). It asks, How does a follower of Jesus live according to God's way? How are you to live in any culture with such an attractive display of God's way of life that it causes praise to God? Jesus' answer: be My influencer. It is a very practical sermon that calls for everyday *faith* obedience in a context heavy on religious *fake* obedience.

This sort of influence does not occur just because one has an important title or a prominent position in a large company or church; it emerges through the attitudes, associations, and activities of any ordinary Christian. When kingdom living occurs by authentic followers of Jesus, the beauty of life under the rule of God is put on display. That's a version of the gospel that spreads because, frankly, there is no better and more attractive way of life!

In His sermon, Jesus used two easy-to-remember images as metaphors of authentic influence in society: salt and light. They are simple. They are ordinary. They are everyday examples. Genius! Salt and light naturally and unapologetically saturate their environments. They make a massive difference to life around them. Every Christian would do well to note what Jesus means when He says that you are the salt of the earth and the light of the world.

You Are the Salt of the Earth

Salt had many uses in the world Jesus first spoke to. We share with that world its primary use: flavoring food. To aid taste was and still is salt's primary use for most. But salt was also used to preserve food right up to the recent invention of refrigerators. Farmers also used salt as a fertilizer for the soil because it facilitates growth by slowing decay. And lastly, salt was a disinfectant; it was an ancient medicine for wounds.

If you are tracking closely with what Jesus is doing here, you get the genius of His choice metaphor for His followers. He is essentially saying that every believer is to be like salt:

- Christians are to *flavor* society, making godliness tasty and pleasant.
- We are to *preserve* society from decay and decline due to sin.
- We are to add those characteristics or nutrients to society that cause it to *flourish*.
- And finally, we are to *heal* a wounded world that is hurt under the abuse of the Evil One.

But the salt metaphor also serves as a warning. Ancient salt dug from pits or from the Dead Sea in Israel wasn't pure like our table salt today. They didn't yet have the processes to remove all the small impurities in what *looked* like a lump of salt. Their lumps of salt had impurities and so could lose saltiness. When it did, it was functionally useless. It was not operating as it should. But remember, Jesus was not really talking about the ins and outs of salt but rather about His followers. He was saying that a Christian who becomes tasteless and does not saturate society with Christ's flavor is not functioning according to his or her true identity and calling.

You Are the Light of the World

The ancient world was very dark after sunset. All you had was the light of an oil lamp or a candle. No electricity meant no light bulbs. Once it went dark, it was *really* dark. You just went to bed, I guess. Access to light at night is a wonderful blessing. Light illuminates its environment. It reveals what is hidden in the dark so that you don't stub your toe or walk into a wall. When light shows up, darkness leaves.

Again, if you are tracking with Jesus' second metaphor, you see He is talking about the value of light—Christians—to a dark society. We help humanity see. Hiding an authentic kingdom lifestyle is like hiding a lit-up city on a hill on a dark night. You can't do it! Jesus went on to talk about how light can be employed both usefully and uselessly. You position lights at home to aid sight. You don't keep lamps hidden in the closet. That would be pointless. Jesus was saying that a genuine Christian is a visible Christian. She or he is to be positioned to help society see life in submission to God, which helps others witness the best and most attractive way of life.

So, both salt and light bless everyday human life. And genuine kingdom living, by everyday followers of Jesus everywhere, does too. It does so naturally and unapologetically.

Actually, *not* to influence, or to compromise in doing so, is abnormal to the Christian life.

Jesus' first sermon to us is simple: Be My influencer. Don't be a tasteless Christian. Don't be a closet Christian. Saturate culture for Christ by influencing those around you. Be Christ's table salt. Be Christ's light bulb!

PROBLEMATIC MYTHS, TRENDS, AND PITFALLS

The twenty-first-century church faces many challenges in living out the call to influence the world for Jesus Christ. But difficulty isn't new; we don't have it worse today than previous generations of Christians. The history of Christianity is one of varying degrees and types of trouble and persecution. But the church has always thrived and defied the many odds stacked against it, and it can continue to do so today.

Unfortunately, internal dangers are emerging; that is, we've let a Trojan horse into the church's fold. No longer are these threats on some distant horizon. They are here, distorting our saltiness and dimming our light. We cannot ignore these myths, trends, and pitfalls. To do so diminishes our saltiness and reduces our brightness for Christ in the world.

Disabling Myths

A type of danger paralyzing our influence in the world is the lies we love to believe; they cripple us. Here are two common ones:

1. **That's just not me.** "I'm not an influencer for God because I'm not a natural leader. Only leaders influence. I'm just an ordinary Christian."

   This is the old fable that only leaders influence and that said leaders are born, not made.[3] That's not true. That mindset reduces what God can do in your life to genetics. It's the excuse God didn't allow Moses to make as he tried to wriggle out of what God was calling him to do with Israel.[4] Your ability to influence those around you does not depend on having a certain personality and charming qualities. It is about the power of Christ in and through you. You *can* become an influencer for Christ. If you are a follower of Jesus, that is your calling.

2. **I'm a nobody.** "I'm not an influencer for God because I've no title, networks, or important position in society. Influencers have followers."

   This is the belief that the only way you can influence someone is from a position of power. This is not true, and it is not the way of Christ. This reduces the boundaries of genuine influence to those with an official title in important places. That's not the Christian understanding of influence. Jesus didn't have an official title. And His own disciples influenced the world mostly from the bottom up. They were ordinary Christians. Without thinking of Christian influence, researchers James Kouzes and Barry Posner conclude the following:

The data clearly challenges the myths that leadership is something that you find only at the highest levels of organizations and society and that it's something reserved for only a handful of charismatic men and women. The notion that there are only a few great people who can lead others to greatness is just plain wrong.[5]

Disturbing Trends

Some troubling patterns we've drifted toward as a church should concern us.

1. **A consumer and spectator church.** A rampant trend in our churches today is consumerism and passivity. For many Christians, Jesus' call on life is restricted to a few Sunday services a month. At these events, we spectate and consume. We watch a service unfold, and if things don't go the way we like, we move on. My goal here is not to guilt anyone. The truth is we've drifted to this state of affairs due to many factors. Perhaps a key cause began with the rise of clergy—setting some people aside full time to serve God on our behalf. This occurred over a thousand years ago and for many good reasons. We do need vocational pastors. But the unintentional result is this: generations of regular Christians are now trained to sit, watch, and busy their lives applying their God-given gifts to other pursuits outside the local church.

2. **A church led by unformed leaders.** This trend worries me as a pastor and a seminary professor. No other significant area of human life would allow it. Churches are increasingly admitting into official leadership positions those who frankly are unfit to lead souls. Can you imagine if the medical profession allowed doctors to practice based simply on passion but not on adequate formation and training? Why is it any different for those who are the doctors of the soul? Yet we—the church, the bride of Christ—can be too quick to appoint as formal leaders combinations of the following:

   i. Those with impressive *credentials* yet untested character and little charisma. Credentials dominate. Competency on paper—usually corporate experience—overrides any other qualification. Issues of the heart are not scrutinized, but this is a key element in what qualifies for formal Christian leadership. It is too often assumed that being the boss over people in the corporate world makes one suitable to be the shepherd of souls.

   ii. Then there are those we appoint who are all *charisma* yet have limited credentials and untested character. In this situation, personality wins. These people are fun, so they get the church vote. Usually, we do this for our youth. If the person is cool or charming (or simply available), then they're in. Recently their qualifications seem to be reduced to the type of jeans they wear, a few tattoos, and a cool beard. Our kids will love them! Now, don't get me wrong. There are many godly servants with beards, tattoos, and winsomeness. I exaggerate here a little to make the point that cultural style and personality can easily override godly substance in leadership selection. There's nothing wrong with being trendy and engaging, but these cannot trump the formation or testing of the heart and faith over time.

iii. Finally, there are those we choose predominantly because of *character* despite limited credentials and little charisma. They are wonderful people. They will do the right thing. We can't say a bad word about them, but it takes more than that to shepherd a flock, though it is the foundation.

Now, I'm not arguing for formal schooling. That doesn't automatically fix anything. Rather, what I am calling for is *formed* influencers over our churches and parachurch ministries. That is, men and women with character *and* charisma *and* credentials, all forged by Christ. This takes time to develop and happens in the context of meaningful and godly relationships. But it's time well spent. It produces the sort of people worth following who can in turn produce influencers just like them in all spheres of life. The long-term health of the church is at stake! Form a leader and leadership happens. Form a godly leader and godly leadership happens. That's authentic influence. Christ and His church deserve the best.

Dangerous Pitfalls

Finally, there are two key traps that cannot be ignored; they are perilous.

1. **A lack of authentic Christian influencers.** This is a growing problem. Our weakening influence for Christ in the world results from not developing Christians to be influencers as God defines influence. A major reason the church is losing influence is because of our skewed understanding of what true influence is.[6] We also seem to be suffering from a severe case of the Dunning-Kruger effect—that is, failing to recognize our limitations and instead thinking we are more able than we actually are. We spend millions on leadership conferences and have plenty of theories on it—great man theories, situational theories, trait theories, and on and on they go.

The problem is that God isn't really consulted. Not seriously. We are relying on culture—often corporate culture—rather than the Scriptures to provide the predominant definition of influence. Yes, there is overlap. But lessons from battlefields and boardrooms, while helpful, cannot overrule the Bible on what constitutes authentic influence in God's eyes.

The Bible doesn't even use the word *leader* that we are so enamored with. The preferred term is *servant*. Abraham was not a business leader but a servant (Genesis 26:24). Joseph was not a prime minister but a servant (Genesis 41:12). Moses wasn't a benevolent dictator but a servant (Deuteronomy 34:5). David wasn't just a king but a servant king (2 Samuel 7:5). Paul wasn't an author, scholar, or world leader but a servant (Romans 1:1). You get the point. Godly influencers are servants who lead whoever is around them toward flourishing in light of God's vision for their lives. That's it! Nothing more. Any resulting title, position, power, or authority is secondary.

Lastly, and important to God, the motivation for godly influence seen in the Scriptures is fidelity, not popularity. It's not about climbing a ladder. The road is usually one of anonymity and obscurity, not celebrity. As Pastor Samuel Chadwick is reputed to have said years ago, "God wants servants, not celebrities." And God's Word shows God's everyday servants how.

2. **The disease of a big ego.** An inflated sense of one's self-importance is a dangerous problem for every Christian. It leads to all sorts of sins, including selfish ambition. We were created to reflect glory, not absorb it. But we have a history of addiction to ourselves.

This common trait flowed through some well-known world influencers—namely, Napoleon, Caesar, and Alexander the Great. I pick these three as examples simply because they tend to be paraded as true influencers. But common to them was an inflated ego that manifested itself as an extreme obsession to be godlike. But let's not be too quick to point the finger at them. It's the same dangerous ego that resides in all of us. The difference is just a matter of dosage and opportunity.

Napoleon Bonaparte (1769–1821) lived to imitate and surpass the accomplishments of his ancient hero, Julius Caesar. Napoleon believed only Caesar equaled him in battlefield skills. And Julius Caesar (100–44 BC) lived to imitate and surpass his ancient hero, Alexander the Great. Caesar is famous for the egotistical words "Veni. Vidi. Vici." ("I came. I saw. I conquered.") to speak of his greatness. It is Caesar who is also reputed to have cried upon encountering a statue of Alexander the Great because his hero had accomplished world domination first—that is, centuries before *and* at a younger age. And then there is Alexander the Great (356–323 BC), who lived to imitate and surpass the accomplishments of his ancient hero, Achilles—a hero in the epic poem by Homer called *The Iliad*. And Achilles was a fictional hero! Upon conquering the world by thirty-two, Alexander also wept that there were no more worlds to conquer.

This infection in the human soul stretches all the way back to Adam and Eve, who were tempted to be like God by that ancient serpent Satan, who also sinned due to his pursuit to be like the Most High (Isaiah 14:14). An inflated ego is an age-old problem. And it remains alive and well.

I was listening in on a conversation at a local coffee shop recently between two chaps sitting at a table beside me. They were regular guys. I wasn't trying to eavesdrop, but it was impossible to avoid hearing them. They had their Bibles on the table and some Christian paraphernalia stuck on their computers and hanging off their backpacks. Then one said to the other, "I should be the next senior pastor of my dad's big church. I could do it. I could be the Big Dawg! Easily. But there is another guy who I think is going to be the 'next guy,' and that is fine, of course. I'm just saying, I'd be awesome." I couldn't believe what I was hearing. The conversation turned into these buddies showering each other with expressions of extreme—no, *supreme*—greatness. All sugarcoated with a form of humble-sounding Christianese. But it was ego, pure and simple. It most certainly remains.

But if we are to be the people of God who shape society for Him according to Christ's way, how do we proceed past these myths, trends, and pitfalls? How are we to learn to be salt and light? The answer lies in the right role models God provides. That is the antidote. God-given role models to copy, to imitate, to aspire to be like. People shape people! God provides several role models for us in the Scriptures, and I'd like to introduce you to one. He was an everyday follower in the grand scheme of things but is God's choice role model for you today: Barnabas.

GOD'S MODEL OF AUTHENTIC INFLUENCE

In the introductory chapter, I argued that human beings are easily shaped and molded. I also claimed that the most powerful influence on a human being is another human being. Human beings are contagious. We rub off on one another. This is potentially delightful *and* dangerous.

I remember teaching my youngest his first words. As a child, he has a built-in and God-designed potential to talk. As a parent, it is my privilege to form, shape, and draw out all his potential. For around six months I worked at teaching him his first word. I'd giggle and laugh with him and whisper in his ear, "Dadda. Dadda." It was a genius plan, and with this child, I started early. After all, I'd failed in getting *Dadda* as the first word from the three kids who came before him. Not with this one. No way! And then one morning the longed-for day arrived. He was ready. He looked me straight in the eye to make sure he had my attention, and as loud and clear as the little guy could make it known, he said, "Mama! Mama!" I whimpered like *I* was the baby. I couldn't believe it. To make it worse, my wife was within earshot! All that to say, shaping another life is delightful *and* dangerous. But shaping others we must. The question is how.

Copying Role Models Is Ancient Discipleship

The ancient model for the formation of a person—what we call discipleship—was *imitatio*. It is essentially this: copy the right role model. That's it! Aspire to be like him or her. Be around the right people. Imitate them. In due time, they rub off on you.

Romans and Jews alike used this model to shape others. They understood the importance of cultivating identity and forming a heart's affections, not just filling a head with information. Essentially, a disciple was one who spent time in the presence of an instructor (let's call him the tutor or rabbi), for they were the embodiment of what they knew and believed. Disciples copied the character, skills, practices, and habits (the lifestyle) of the person they wanted to become. Ancient wisdom believed *showing* others how to live was more effective than *telling* them how to live.

Many ancient writers testified to this and also gave warnings concerning whom to pick as your pattern to copy. Seneca the Younger in the first century AD wrote, "The living voice and the intimacy of the common life will help you more than the written word. You must go to the scene of the action first, because men put more faith in their eyes than in their ears, and second, because the way is long if one follows precepts, but short and helpful, if one follows patterns."[7]

The great Cicero, a century before Seneca, similarly said to "show the student whom he should imitate, and in such a way that he may copy with care the chief qualities of his model. Let practice then follow, whereby in his imitation he may represent the exact resemblance of him whom he chose as his pattern. . . . But he who shall proceed right, must first of all be very careful in making his choice."[8]

This approach was not just the wisdom of the faith*less* (the pagans) but also the faith*ful*. If you think this *imitatio* thing is all secular stuff, look at the following statements by the apostle Paul in the New Testament:

- *Imitate* me, just as I also *imitate* Christ (1 Corinthians 11:1 NKJV)
- Be *imitators* of me (Philippians 3:17 NET)

- You became *imitators* of us and of the Lord
  (1 Thessalonians 1:6 NET)
- You know yourselves how you must *imitate* us
  (2 Thessalonians 3:7 NET)
- Be *imitators* of God (Ephesians 5:1 NET)

And let's not ignore that *imitatio* is what Jesus did with the Twelve for years. Their formation began with a call: "Come, follow me" (Matthew 4:19). It then progressed to regular life lived simply and side by side for years.

The bottom line is this: making disciples is about remolding the heart after the image of Christ in light of truth and in the power of the Spirit through meaningful relationships with the right role models, all to the glory of the Father. It's an ancient, tested, and effective way to shape a life. It takes time, and it takes copying the right role model.

Copying God's Role Model Is Relevant Discipleship

As we will discover throughout this book, the life and actions of Barnabas *show* us rather than *tell* us how to influence our patch of the world for Jesus Christ. In watching this everyday disciple, we learn how to disciple. Copying him is like receiving an antidote to the myths, trends, and pitfalls we discussed earlier. He does not present a how-to *method* but a how-to *model*. It is a practical and accessible way for any ordinary believer—like you and me—to influence culture for Jesus Christ.

And such an influence begins precisely where you are. Research shows that a family member is by far the most formative role model in the lives of others. That's right, those already in your daily life. The summary of the results of this research shows you who is the most likely influence on a person within a certain age bracket.[9]

Respondents between eighteen and thirty are influenced most by a:

- Family member (40 percent)
- Teacher or coach (26 percent)
- Community or religious leader (11 percent)
- Business leader (7 percent)
- Political leader (4 percent)
- Professional athlete (3 percent)
- Entertainer/movie star (2 percent)
- None/not sure/other (7 percent)

Respondents over thirty are influenced most by a:

- Family member (46 percent)
- Teacher or coach (14 percent)
- Community or religious leader (8 percent)
- Business leader (23 percent)
- Political leader (4 percent)
- Professional athlete (.5 percent)
- Entertainer/movie star (.5 percent)
- None/not sure/other (4 percent)

If you have family, you shape them more than you know. Teachers, coaches, pastors, and celebrities don't come close to shaping a family member the way you can.

All that said, here is our first principle to adopt. It is a general one, a mindset to switch on. The rest that emerges from the life of Barnabas in the chapters that follow are how-to expressions of accomplishing this first one.

. . . .

BARNABAS PRINCIPLE #1: INFLUENCE

A godly influencer saturates any and every environment for God. That's God's will for *your* life—that you be an everyday influencer for Jesus Christ.

. . . .

THE BARNABAS WAY THROUGH YOU

Godly influence matters. We need it in all areas of life, be it government, business, education, leisure, church, or home. All followers of Jesus are called to be like tasty table salt and bright spotlights everywhere they go. You can flavor culture for Jesus. You can reveal Him to the world.

This can occur irrespective of your placement in life—CEO, mom, dad, pastor, unemployed, student, retired, teacher, and on and on the list goes. Barnabas can show you how. He understood how to make disciples. He knew that you influence others for God by injecting yourself into their lives. You rub off on them by being close. You have many people in your immediate sphere of influence. Barnabas models for you an accessible, doable, biblical, grassroots portrait of the everyday authentic influencer God wants you to become.

Some Food for Thought

BEFORE ANSWERING THE FOLLOWING QUESTIONS, reflect on (or perhaps revisit again) the ideas developed in the main sections of this chapter.

1. List those areas in your day-to-day life where you come into natural contact with others. Remember, these are sacred ministry spaces—opportunities for influence. Begin to view them as such!

2. Revisit Jesus' teaching in Matthew 5:13–14 on salt and light. Think about the characteristics of these items as they speak into your call to influence those around you. What is involved in being Christ's salt and light in your day-to-day life? How could this be accomplished?

3. Revisit the myths, trends, and pitfalls presented in this chapter. Do any of these dangers show up in your life? If you are a ministry leader, reflect and discuss with others the dangers these present for the twenty-first-century church. Are there others?

CHAPTER 2

Dreamers and Doers

Hands-On Vision

Your kingdom come, your will be done,
on earth as it is in heaven.
JESUS

Not much happens without a dream.
ROBERT K. GREENLEAF

THE BRITISH TEA BREAK—THAT MID-MORNING PAUSE in the day. It's a daily mass migration of the British workforce at 11 a.m. (aka elevenses). Desk chairs screech across office floors. Builders climb off scaffolding and hop into their work vans. Call centers ignore ringing phones and factory floors go silent. Only the electrical grid gets a surge of work during elevenses as electric kettles boil in sync across the land. A symbol of the United Kingdom is reborn every day as a hot cup of tea with a splash of milk and, if you're really lucky, a biscuit or two (think cookies) to escort the tea down. It's fifteen minutes of daily British bliss.

Then there is the tank. Not a water tank, an oil tank, an oxygen tank, or a tank top (as in clothing) but rather the military tank (aka landships). The one that carries a gun barrel on its face like a long, protruding nose. The tank was the mechanical warhorse of twentieth-century warfare. It dominated battlefields and changed the history of human warfare. Its tactical use even won wars.

Finally, consider the onesie (aka the siren suit), that one-piece item of clothing we wrap babies in to keep them warm and cute. Adults still hope onesies come into fashion for them, too, one day. The thing is, the onesie once *was* adult attire.

That's right, the original onesies were for grown-ups, not kids. Oh, that those days would return!

Elevenses. Landships. Onesies. What on earth would these three have in common? The answer is quite simple. They are siblings; they share the same dad: Winston S. Churchill. That's right! The great British prime minister and liberator of the Western world during World War II played a key role in birthing them all. Or so it is thought (paternity tests are inconclusive). Churchill even met US President Roosevelt and Soviet Union leader General Stalin at an important summit sporting a onesie and smoking his trademark cigar!

Winston Churchill is a remarkable figure in history. Whether you like him or not, he grabs attention. He was a journalist, a bestselling author, a historian, a soldier, a painter, an inventor, a public speaker, and, of course, a global influencer (even a fashion influencer with his top hat and cigar poses, all before the days of Instagram!). It is no wonder that in 2002 Churchill was deemed the greatest Briton of all time.[1] That said, it's a miracle he ever made anything of his life at all. His early failures and disappointments are vast. Perhaps hardest of all to overcome was living in the shadow of his famous father, Randolph Churchill—a bossy statesman. Randolph was so obsessed with himself that he had little time or affection for his son. Bizarrely, in the story of the greatest Briton of all time—and British history is a long, long time—daddy issues abound.

How did this individual shape so much of modern British life in ways large and small? What stands out about this man?

At the risk of oversimplifying, the answer is twofold. Churchill had two indispensable traits that resulted in the vast influence he exerted over his immediate world. First, he was visionary. Churchill saw the potential world needing to be birthed (in warfare, in clothing, in workers' tea-break rights, in the famous National Health Service of the UK, and on and on). And second, Churchill was practical. He saw to it that this potential world *would* be birthed. Churchill dreamed big and worked hard. He was a dreamer *and* a doer.

TRANSLATING GREAT DREAMS INTO REALITY

Authentic influence involves vision *and* action.

All good things begin with a vision. This picture of a potential world in the mind's eye is the first step toward birthing the world soon to be. If there had been no visionary picture of an easy-to-put-on, single-piece item of clothing during the cold nights of Nazi bomb raids over London in World War II, there would be no siren suit to wear when the alarms went off. If there were no siren suits, there would be no warm and cute onesies for our babies today. As the leadership expert Robert Greenleaf said, "Not much happens without a dream. And for something great to happen, there must be a great dream. Behind every great achievement is a dreamer of great dreams."[2] It all begins with a vision; it starts with dreaming those great dreams!

But without action, vision is just daydreaming. Yes, the ability to see that potential world is essential. It sets a goal to pursue—a world to create and then enter and inhabit. But without rolling up the sleeves and getting to work (without blueprints, clothes patterns, even prototypes), that potential world can't become a reality. It all just remains a nice and happy "what if"; it stays as nothing more than a great but dead idea.

Both vision and action are essential to have genuine influence on people. Without vision, our actions wander aimlessly. Without action, our vision withers into forgetfulness. Dreams must be turned into reality. In fact, to have an authentic impact on anything or anyone is precisely "the capacity to translate vision into reality."[3] When visionary Christians are also practical, more than national tea breaks, tanks, and onesies are born—better worlds begin to emerge for those around you.

Godly influencers need both vision and action. We must be dreamers *and* doers.

THE BARNABAS WAY

Followers of Jesus Christ have a wonderful calling—a Great Commission—to bring God's vision for His world into reality on earth. Thy kingdom come! It doesn't matter what arena of life God has you in. You are God's everyday believer who gets to influence those workmates, that campus, those kids, your neighborhood, that church for Jesus—be it one person or a thousand people in your entire life. That's your responsibility.

And grander outcomes than Churchill's national elevens and onesies can result when one life is influenced for God. All to say, you've got a call from God to be a dreamer and a doer.

And you really can be that dreamer and doer. Even you! You dream and do all the time. Every human being is naturally quite visionary; we are all anticipation machines that spend much time imagining our lives in situations that do not yet exist.[4] We daydream of sitting in cars we don't yet own and decorating homes we don't yet possess. We vacation in distant resorts we've never visited. We certainly know how to dream. And we know how to do. If you're honest, you'll admit that your life gets aligned in the practical pursuit of your visions of that very "good life" you dreamed up. We roll up our sleeves to pursue it with hours and hours and hours of work. We spend hard-earned cash birthing that good life. Our visions of the good life tend to cost money—lots of money. And we spend it in that pursuit.

The problem, of course, is the visions of the good life we tend to pursue are often selfishly skewed. Our fixations on imaginary versions of our potential lives are based on what the culture around us sows in our hearts without thought for God. It's not always God's vision for us or His version of the good life. The result? Selfish pursuits untethered from God's vision for our lives in the world. Now, that's dangerous to you!

Barnabas, however, shows us a better way. He shows us God's way; even better, he shows us an *accessible* pathway to God's way. He caught God's vision for the world and made it the good life to pursue.

God Dreams and God Does

God has a vision for His world. He dreams of what will be. The story of the Scriptures shows us where God's been heading all along. The Bible articulates not only God's dream but also His doings that guarantee its reality, and this despite Satan's hijacking maneuver. Of course, the only way of catching God's vision is if you read His version of life. The Bible is not just a map of history but also a compass for navigating life well. It steers our lives according to God's vision of the good life for the sake of the world around us.

Barnabas caught this vision. Here's a condensed version of God's dreaming and doings to orient you. Immersing yourself in Scripture will give you the full account.

In the beginning, God created the heavens and the earth: a kingdom (Genesis 1–2). This realm (the earth) with a rule of life (God's law) for all creatures (subjects) managed by God's "lookalikes" (human beings) and with Him (in fellowship) was God's dream turned into His creative doings. It was a kingdom of heaven on earth. It not only expressed His glory—His unequaled Being—but, when it operated as He designed, it also ascribed glory right back at Him. A tree waving in the wind, a fish swimming in the sea, a smile on a human face all declare praise to God by His creative design.

Now that ancient serpent Satan was craftier than any of the wild animals God made (Genesis 3). While unable to make God's "lookalikes" rebel, Satan tempted our first mom and dad to choose to do so. In rebelling against God, Adam and Eve not only mocked God's glory but subjected the kingdom under their care—and all who would follow—to sin and Satan. That is, we turned God's kingdom here into an existence in rebellion to God. The consequence of choosing life without God is death—eternal death. Deservedly and justly so!

But God so loved the world that He gave His only begotten Son (Genesis 3–Revelation 20). The Scriptures reveal bit by bit that God's dreams and doings were not derailed by our betrayal and partnership with Satan. The history of buying humanity back, while motivated by love (God does love you!), is also motivated by God's restoring His own glory. The death, burial, and resurrection of Jesus Christ is God's dealing with death and sin without compromising His own integrity, justice, and glory. Those who look to His mode of salvation—faith alone in Jesus Christ alone—receive eternal life His way, the only way. And this is good news for all to embrace: this is the gospel!

And now a new heaven and a new earth appear on the horizon of history (Revelation 21–22). It is back to life in a new earth (realm) under God's rule (God's law) for all (subjects) governed under the God-man Jesus Christ (the ruling King) and we with Him (in fellowship). This is still God's dream and doings: a kingdom of heaven on earth. It is a climactic and beautiful expression of God's glory—His unequaled Being. And this renewed chorus of glory to Him will continue with no end. This is the gospel!

Barnabas Pursued God's Dreams and Doings

Barnabas saw the world as God wants to make it. He saw where God is heading in history. In light of that, he made God's vision of the good life his personal dream to pursue.

Every follower of Jesus must do the same. Influence in your little corner of the world begins there. This is precisely why Barnabas's account is given to us in the book of Acts—he is a role model for followers of Jesus. Don't read past this too fast; let it sink in. At the risk of belaboring the point, let me say it again. Barnabas's story is intentionally placed in the Scriptures *for you to copy.* God is giving us a very concrete example to imitate. Barnabas shows (not tells) every believer in Jesus Christ what it looks like to live out God's dreams in a local community, in a home, in a church, in that neighborhood, in that relationship. He is God's choice pick for you. We meet him for the first time with this in mind in Acts 4:36–37:

> Joseph, a Levite from Cyprus, whom the apostles called Barnabas (which means "son of encouragement"), sold a field he owned and brought the money and put it at the apostles' feet.

There is a lot packed into these short introductory verses. We have a man, whose name isn't even Barnabas, who sells farmland and then gives the proceeds from the sale to the apostles of the first church in Jerusalem. While there is lots there, it doesn't seem like a big deal. Well, it is! We'll examine these details in a few moments. What is essential for you to catch at this point is some context and structure. I know, that sounds somewhat boring. Who wants structure? But if we want to grasp why God includes Barnabas in His Word here for you, it is essential we examine why he shows up when he does.

Barnabas is introduced in the context of a description of life inside the early church—the first local church. We get a snapshot of how a community of early believers acted and related within their church in Jerusalem.

Those initial days and months following the departure of Jesus were exciting and tough. The Holy Spirit arrived. The church was born. The good news—the gospel—spread throughout Jerusalem, to the surrounding regions of Judea and Samaria, and then to the ends of the earth. "Life with God is available again" is great news to proclaim! Thousands became followers of Jesus. But this didn't sit well with those Jewish leaders who recently thought they had gotten rid of Jesus. As a result, persecution in Jerusalem continued, albeit now against His followers. And in those tricky times, Christians who looked to God in faith looked after one another in love. Barnabas is introduced in the context of a look inside that church family during tough times. He looked after others in love because he looked to God in faith.

The structure of the broader scene in which he emerges in Acts 4:32–5:16 is important to the point God makes. How we meet Barnabas helps us see why God wants us to meet him. We see a summary of life inside the church and an emphasis on growth in unity (4:32–35). Then we're shown two examples of the types of members in that church (4:36–5:11). We return once again to another summary of life inside the church but now with a focus on its growth in numbers (5:12–16). Basically, the two summaries that frame the entire section make sure you understand that we're talking about life inside Jerusalem

Community Church. While times were tough on the outside, God was growing His church in unity and in numbers on the inside.

But the two specific examples within these scenes show us the types of believers inside this first church that we are all potentially like: one positive, one negative. Barnabas is introduced as the positive role model to copy in whatever local church, culture, and century God places any believer: he is our template. Ananias and Sapphira are the opposite—a warning. Don't be like them! This structural contrast forces believers to ask themselves, What type of influence am I most like to those around me? Am I like Barnabas or the married couple, Ananias and Sapphira?

How we meet Barnabas in the context of church life makes a point: the Barnabas way is there for us to copy if we are to be positive members of our local church. And from the details of what *is* said concerning him within those few verses (Acts 4:36–37) emerge our next two principles for everyday believers to adopt.

The Barnabas Way Is Vision-Driven

If you recall, vision is that picture in your mind of an ideal potential world. It's the ability to see that far-off horizon and to begin aligning life in that direction. Too many followers of Jesus (and too many Christians who are in leadership) have a foggy vision of God's version of the good life. This affects the present world they inhabit *and* the one they build for others around them. That was not Barnabas. In these introductory verses, we see that Barnabas had clearly seen the world through God's eyes. Because of that, he aligned his life according to God's pursuits in the lives of those beside him. God's vision for the church was Barnabas's personal vision to pursue. That's why God uses him as an illustration for us.

BARNABAS PRINCIPLE #2: *VISION*

A godly influencer sees through God's eyes.

What I'm saying is that Barnabas understood the teaching of the book in which we find him. Now, that is a remarkable thought. Think about it. Barnabas didn't read the book of Acts, but his life certainly is a testimony to its teaching.

The book of Acts is a record of the activities of the Holy Spirit through this new humanity birthed in Jesus Christ: the church. It's a vision document. But it's also a mission document. It is an account of God's plan for the church and the early execution of it in the world despite ongoing opposition. God was at work in and through His church in this age of history as His dream unfolded according to His master plan. And it is an age we're still in! Barnabas is a positive example of the progress made—just an ordinary member of the church who did his little bit among those around him as he was led by God.

Barnabas lived in light of God's vision. He saw the local church as a display of God's glory in any little patch of the world in which it is found—an advertisement of life under the rule of God. He saw the church as a display that invited others into that life. Perhaps it was Barnabas who helped the apostle Paul understand his own writing in Ephesians 3:10–11, which shows how the church shows off God's glory to His enemies. If this display is to shine forth, then it must be switched on. Barnabas understood that. He was a light bulb that was switched on. Why? Because he caught and bought in to God's vision for the world. And remembering Ananias and Sapphira, we know that not all followers of Jesus are switched on.

God's vision for the world through the church remains His vision for you as a member of that same church. We live in the same stage of history that Barnabas lived in. Sure, it is a few thousand years on down history's timeline, but it is still the church age. God still wants to display His glory through us despite the opposition we face. We get to bring His dreams into reality. The way you do this is open before you, even though it is bound by the parameters of His Word. Nothing will help you more in catching God's vision for your life than poring over His vision in His Word. All of us can do that.

Some years ago I was preaching a sermon on knowing God through the Scriptures when I came across a story told by a well-known preacher of yesteryear, Pastor Harry Ironside. It caught my attention initially because it related Pastor Ironside's encounter with a man from my motherland, Northern Ireland. The man was ill. He lived in California in a small tent under some olive trees near Pastor Ironside's family home. It is a moving story for many reasons but particularly for the way it speaks of how available God is anywhere and at any time to share His vision with whoever is willing to take the time to listen. Here's what Ironside wrote about the encounter in that small tent:

> I can remember how my heart was touched as I looked down upon his thin worn face upon which I could see the peace of Heaven clearly manifested. His name was Andrew Fraser. He could barely speak above a whisper, for his lungs were almost gone, but I can recall how, after a few words of introduction, he said to me, "Young man, you are trying to preach Christ; are you not?" I replied, "Yes, I am." "Well," he whispered, "sit down a little, and let us talk together about the Word of God." He opened his well-worn Bible, and until his strength was gone, simply, sweetly, and earnestly he opened up truth after truth as he turned from one passage to another, in a way that my own spirit had never entered into them. Before I realized it, tears were running down my face, and I asked, "Where did you get these things? Could you tell me where I could find a book that would open them up to me? Did you learn these things in some seminary or college?" I shall never forget his answer: "My dear young man, I learned these things on my knees on the mud floor of a little sod cottage in the north of Ireland. There, with my open Bible before me, I used to kneel for hours at a time and ask the Spirit of God to reveal Christ to my soul and to open the Word to my heart, and He taught me more on my knees on that mud floor than I ever could have learned in all the seminaries or colleges in the world." It was not many weeks after this that he was absent from the body and present with

the Lord, but the memory of that visit has always remained with me and is a most precious recollection. Is it not true that most of us simply do not stay long enough in the presence of God?[5]

God's vision of the good life is accessible in His Word. And God Himself is available to guide you in it. Barnabas caught this vision in the first century. His life testifies to the message contained within it. Andrew Fraser did, too, in the nineteenth century—and he did so on a mud floor of a cold and damp sod cottage in Northern Ireland. And we can access it in our comfortable surroundings. When we do, we can become godly influencers who see the world around us as God wants to make it.

A godly influencer sees through God's eyes—that is, through what is revealed in His Word. An authentic life of influence is rooted in God's Word.

The Barnabas Way Is Active and Practical

Vision expresses itself in mission. Those who "get" God get to work. The previous principle on vision emerged in light of Barnabas's alignment and incarnation of the movements of the whole book of Acts—and the story of Scripture! Only those who catch that vision will live out this next principle in the details of Acts 4:36–37. Barnabas was that type of person. He wasn't just an optimistic futurist, a dreamer. He was very much a present pragmatist, a doer. Barnabas showed us three accessible and hands-on ways you can express God's heart toward those around you.

First, Barnabas was generous with his words. This is perhaps what he is best known for today—words of encouragement. The reason for this legacy is understandable. It is the reputation he had in the early church too. The name we know him by, Barnabas, is a nickname, not his birth name. The name his mom gave him, Joseph, is a pretty good name if you are a Jew. But the early

> **BARNABAS PRINCIPLE #3:**
> ***ACTION***
>
> A godly influencer serves as God's hands given God's heart.

church found one more suited to *this* Joseph, and that's what stuck. And while nicknames then, like today, could be cruel, they could also be complimentary. Barnabas is a nickname of high praise; it is a compliment—son of encouragement. Here is one whose words put a spring in another's step, a smile on a face, and hope in others' hearts. So, let's forget Joseph (sorry, Mom) and go with Barnabas. That's what he is to us. Others in this church fellowship might have been "Mr. Pain in the Neck" or "Mrs. Moan and Groan," but not this guy. He was "Mr. Encouragement." And let's not ignore that he was nicknamed Barnabas by the apostles. Such was his reputation in the eyes of God's chosen leaders.

You see, encouragement matters. What a great legacy it is to be known as an encourager. We underestimate this ministry to others. But think about this: It is estimated that on average a human will speak around 860 million words in their lifetime.[6] And we know through the wisdom of the ages, and our own experiences, that our tongue can heal or hurt. Proverbs 12:18, for example, tells us that words can be like the thrusts of a sword (ouch!) or that which brings healing. The well-known essayist Mark Twain is reputed to have said, "I can live two months on one good compliment." He's right! And the opposite is also true. Careless words linger on like a bad smell. While the tongue can be hard to tame, as the apostle James warned in his letter, godly influencers must resolve to put it to good use.

All that to say, a man who has a ministry and reputation as an encourager to those around him is a remarkable person: he is a role model. And all you need to join him in that influential ministry is a tongue, a *tamed* tongue. So, first, Barnabas was generous with his words. A practical step toward authentic influence over those around you is generosity in speech.

Second, Barnabas was generous with his wallet. Of the many things that could be said of Barnabas, God wants the record to show that our role model was generous with his stuff. That's as practical as it gets: sacrificial giving. He owns a piece of farmland—presumably on the island of Cyprus—and he sold it. He didn't just think of selling it. He didn't just plan to sell it one day or leave it as part of his estate. He actually sold it. Why? Because there were needs in the lives of those around him. That's the context of this section of Acts. Who knows, perhaps all those kids in Sunday school causing a ruckus are noisy because they're hungry. "Let's go buy some food," Barnabas would say. The proceeds from the sale of his land may have eased the burdens of those around him. After all, God's people were his family.

This sacrificial giving is precisely what is emphasized most in this section. The contrast with Ananias and Sapphira makes this clear. They, too, were Christians in that same local church. They, too, owned land. They, too, sold land and gave. But Barnabas gave generously, while Ananias and Sapphira wanted to *appear* generous. God wouldn't have that! True generosity is the fruit of gratitude. Generosity is a virtue rooted in God and His vision of the good life. Greed is not. Barnabas was generous with his stuff because he served a God who is generous—with His stuff *and* with His Son.

Some years ago, I sat across the table over lunch with a wonderful man of God that I had the honor of calling Uncle Stanley. He was in his eighties then and had been—and is—a very successful businessman. For decades, he supported my parents on the mission field in Spain. In fact, I don't remember not knowing Uncle Stanley. Now, as an adult, I could relate to him in a different way—adult to adult. It was a wonderful conversation. He told me about life in Belfast in years past. He told me about coming to know Christ. And then through tears, he told me how as a young man he longed to serve God on the mission field. In fact, he pleaded with God to send him as a missionary, but God said no. God wanted him to send others to foreign lands. And that is precisely what Uncle Stanley devoted his life to do. His entire business empire is God's and God's alone. All his stuff is God's stuff, so it is given to His work in the world. Beautiful. And then, through tears, he said,

"Jonathan, sadly the last part of man to get saved, if ever, is his wallet."

Not so with Barnabas. In a world—then and now—where the motto is "Get! Get! Get!" Barnabas's was "Give! Give! Give!" Barnabas understood that the antidote to greed is generosity. He understood that when a person is saved by God, that includes his or her wallet. That's still the case. And God wants that on the record of His choice role model Barnabas. You see, God doesn't reward those who appear on the rich lists or get to the end of life with the most money in their accounts. The secular culture celebrates that. Rather, God rewards those who embrace the mission of being faithful stewards of His stuff. And so Barnabas was generous with his wallet. Your authentic influence will spread to those around you when you are generous with your stuff—God's stuff!

Third, Barnabas was generous in his walk. Barnabas pursued a walk of humility, selflessness, and self-abandon. He gave of himself, not just of his stuff. We'll see this as the chapters unfold. But we see it here in these verses as well, and I'm not just talking about giving money and land. I'm talking about status. Barnabas gave up his high standing in the structures of that culture. He didn't climb up the ladder of perceived importance; he chose to climb down. Let me explain.

Barnabas was a Levite from Cyprus. There is a reason we are told this piece of information. He not only was a true Jew named after one of Israel's historic heroes (Joseph) but was of the tribe of the Levites. In the Jewish way of viewing the world, including their own nation, the Levites were an elite tribe.

They were that tribe chosen to represent God from within the chosen nation of all nations in the world—an elite tribe in an elite nation! Levites occupied the places of high standing in Israel.

But we also need to go back to that farmland he sold to fully grasp the extent of the point at hand. Back then, only a few in the world owned land. Everyone else just worked the land for those few owners. And those landowning elite made all important life decisions for the rest. Landowners ruled the lives of all other people. They alone made governing decisions. And you couldn't get your hands on a piece of land too easily. No one would give it up without a fight considering the status it conferred. There were no real estate offices you could walk into and inquire about a purchase. There were no online listings. There was no open real estate market. The minority who owned land sold it at great cost to themselves: the cost was status. It cost them a seat at the table of importance in that world's structures.

Barnabas didn't just give money here. Barnabas gave up his high position in that culture. And what's more, he allowed former fishermen now turned preaching apostles to decide how to spend what he gave! He was submissive to those above him in God's structures of the church. (And all God's pastors said "Amen!") He pursued humility, not high status. Authentic Christian influence flows from you when humility is evident in you; it is an attractive trait—a Christlike quality.

Barnabas was very much like the Austrian nobleman Count Nicolas von Zinzendorf (1700–1760). Zinzendorf also spent his wealth generously on those around him, particularly in the support of spreading the gospel across the world. He, too, encouraged believers and had a godly self-awareness of his standing in the world despite his aristocratic title. And like Barnabas, the reason for doing so was simple. Referring to Jesus, Zinzendorf said, "I have one passion: it is He, He alone."

A godly influencer serves as God's hands. Generosity of words, wallet, and walk follows those who catch God's vision.

THE BARNABAS WAY THROUGH YOU

Vision casts before us a desired future. Action delivers it. Both are essential and come in that specific order in the lives of authentic influencers: vision *then* action. The French writer and war hero Antoine de Saint-Exupéry captured this well: "If you want to build a ship, don't drum up people to collect wood and don't assign them tasks and work, but rather teach them to long for the endless immensity of the sea."[7] That's true. We will busy ourselves with God's doings in the world if we catch His dreams for the world from His Word.

Barnabas did just that. His actions testify to a man who longed for God's version of the good life. His very nickname indicates he was busy at this long before his story went public in the Bible. His life shows you his heart. If you want to see what vision of the good life you are pursuing, it's easy to check. Take a look at your calendar, your monthly spending, and the hours you devote to one week's activities. Where your time, money, and energy go is exactly where your heart is. We all live out of what our heart values.

Barnabas valued God. He was a dreamer of great dreams—God's dreams. And he was an active participant in translating God's vision down on earth. He was a dreamer and a doer. Barnabas had what contemporary experts would call emotional intelligence (EQ). There are lots of types of intelligence, and Barnabas modeled many of these.[8] In these introductory verses, we see he had a high EQ. He understood the heart of God. He was empathetic to the plight of those around him. And, therefore, he was able to make good decisions in light of both.

It is God's desire that Christians like you cultivate this too. You are to be a dreamer of God's dreams and a doer for God. It will require regular time with Him in His Word and active participation in His activities in the world. Then you can live as Barnabas did with an authentic life of influence. You really can be the answer to Jesus' prayer request in Matthew 6:10: "Your kingdom come, your will be done, on earth as it is in heaven."

Some Food for Thought

REMEMBER, BEFORE ANSWERING THE QUESTIONS that follow, it is helpful to think and talk your way through the main truths from the sections in this chapter.

1. Think through God's vision for His world and what He is doing about it. Can you articulate it in your own words?

2. Barnabas incarnated God's vision for the church in his day in practical ways. How can you express God's dreams and doings to those around you?

3. Authentic believers, and certainly servant leaders like pastors, lead those around them by modeling the pursuit of God's version of the good life. This requires emotional intelligence: understanding the heart of God *and* the needs of people. How do you nurture this in your own life regularly?

CHAPTER 3

Hinges and Bridges

Detecting Potential Even in Risky People

Forgive us our sins, for we also forgive everyone who sins against us.
JESUS

You good guy or bad guy?
JAMES (TWO-YEAR-OLD)

JONATHAN, DID YOU READ *HOW THE IRISH SAVED Civilization*?"

"Eh . . . that's funny Mike, very funny," I replied somewhat sarcastically.

I continued to sip at my coffee, waiting for the punchline on the next Irish joke. I'm from Northern Ireland. I've heard them all. I thought he was about to launch into the old joke I've heard many times before:

Why did God invent whiskey?

So that the Irish wouldn't rule the civilized world!

Mike and I met early every Thursday morning—very early. He took me under his wing while I was in seminary. He was convinced God could do something with my life, though I wasn't so sure. But Mike bought me nice coffee. And I liked that he believed in me. So I was happy to drag myself out of bed early and see what Mike launched my way.

From an outsider's view, our weekly conversations would appear very disjointed. We talked about anything and everything. Yet nothing could be further from the truth. Mike knew precisely what he was doing. Mike was an artist. Like a potter, he had a vision in his head and was shaping my heart with that in mind. Early every Thursday morning Mike was sculpting my heart after the image of the Lord Jesus

Christ. This was authentic discipleship. Mike was a restoration artist.

"I'm serious," Mike declared. "This isn't a joke. The Irish saved our Western world."

For a moment, I was strangely flattered. Like I was somehow sort of a hero by association. But that was ridiculous, so I caught myself and just chuckled again at the thought. Not the philosophy of the Greeks. Not the law and order of the Romans. Not French refinements or German engineering. But my lot—the Irish—*we* saved Western life? Surely, Mike was having a laugh. That's got to be a joke!

"Give me a break, Mike," I laughed. "We're known for lots of stuff, but not for saving the civilized world."

But Mike didn't crack a smile. Before I could object, we were in his car heading toward the local bookstore. And there it was. Close to the entrance and prominently displayed: *How the Irish Saved Civilization* by Thomas Cahill, a national bestseller.[1] History, not fiction. History, not comedy. Was this bookstore—and the entire world—in on Mike's joke?

I got home and read the book in one go. I was glued. It was no joke! It appears the Western world was plundered, pillaged, and burned to ashes a long time ago. All records of humanity's advancements were gone. Think about that. All we knew of science, technology, engineering, medicine, education—all of it gone up in smoke. All records of humankind's literature, activities, and wisdom up to the fifth century AD were gone (history, poetry, law, government, and all knowledge of the existence of humanity's heroes—Aristotle, Alexander the Great, Julius

Caesar, Jesus). All records went up in a puff of smoke when the barbarian hordes burned the institutions, libraries, and cities of the Roman world—the West. *All* was gone!

Well, all except for the copies of that literature stored in cold and damp monasteries clinging to cliffs on the edge of the known world: Ireland. The barbarians didn't bother to go there. No one did. To the sound of seagulls squawking and seals barking on rugged shorelines like Skellig Michael, monks huddled in stone towers and copied, copied, copied all humankind's works. It's known as the Green Martyrdom: Irish (green) monks devoting their lives to God (martyrdom) by preserving and transmitting texts. It was their life of worship! And so, eventually, all that they copied flowed back into Europe as though it was downloaded from an ancient iCloud. Like the proverbial phoenix rising from the ashes, humanity's collective knowledge thus far—I repeat, all of it, from Cicero (rhetoric) to Virgil (poetry) to Homer (poetry) to Aristotle (philosophy) to Herodotus (history) to Tacitus (history) to the Bible (truth) to Jesus (the Son of God) and on and on—was resurrected from the grave. And who knows how much we *did* lose?

All that to say, the door of Western civilization swung back open again because its hinge was the grueling copying work of Irish monks. Without those human hinges in that activity, that door would remain shut. But these unknown "nobodies" were more than just a one-off pivot point whose copying swiveled open that door. They went further than that. To use another helpful metaphor, they also became the human bridges that civilization used to repeatedly cross back over to old shores.

Mike wanted me to see that. Perhaps another everyday Northern Irishman could be useful to God in the world again. I could open doors of opportunity for others. I could also build bridges for others to walk across.

HISTORY TWISTS AND TURNS THROUGH PEOPLE

History flows like a meandering river. And while its course is directed by God, He's chosen to involve people in its many twists and turns. People—Irish monks, Mike, Dad—affect the direction of the lives of others in differing ways. Directly or indirectly, our decisions, plans, actions, and reactions shape those around us—for better or worse. Yes, God directs history, but His hand often does so through human hands.

The doors of opportunity that others walk through hinge open on human shoulders. But people can be more than one-off aids in the lives of others. We can become the bridges they regularly walk across. We can be like Mickey Davis, one of the greatest heroes of World War II. You've never heard of this regular man, but what an impact he had.

It's 1940 and Nazi bombs rain down on London every night. Think about that. It was horrible. It's dark due to mandatory blackouts. It's noisy from sirens, anti-aircraft guns, explosions, and human shrieks. It's scary because there's nowhere safe for many people to go.

Some try to squeeze into shelters at local hotels, but these are small. Others cram into Tube (subway) stations, but these aren't safe—fifty people were blown to pieces in a station on one occasion. In the East End of London, the basement of the Fruit and Wool Exchange building becomes a go-to place for some. It becomes a bedroom for around five thousand people. That is double the standing capacity it can hold. Down there it is also dark and noisy—mostly kids crying given the bombing above. The floor they all lie on is dirty from the five thousand people hunkered down there the night before. And it smells. No, it stinks! There are no loos (think restrooms). That's what the stench is: human waste. It's hell on earth above and now hell below too—*every* night.

And here, in that dark and smelly mass basement-bedroom, is where Mickey Davis makes his impact. Mickey doesn't live up to the stereotypes of what an influencer in the world should be. He's not a decorated soldier. He's not a seasoned politician. He's not an executive in a complex organization. He's just an optician (no offense, opticians) whose office was blown to pieces in the streets above. Oh, and he's only twenty-nine years old, is hunchbacked, and stands less than four feet tall, hence the affectionate (though now improper) nickname, Mickey the Midget. Yet the door to a better life for thousands in London swung open on the hinge that was this ordinary, next-to-nobody little man.

Here's why. It's simple, really. Mickey looked at what was going on around him and took a risk to change the direction of its flow, just as my friend Mike had done for me. Mickey saw that something needed to be done for the security of all those people in that dark and smelly basement. It was fast becoming the "Wild West" of the East End—literally an underground world of crime. Mickey organized a basement police force and brought in a judge. And then there were all those kids. The children couldn't sleep due to noise and fear, so Mickey organized music and games followed by bedtime stories to tuck them all in at night. He established a medical unit with supplies and medical staff. He organized food donations, bedding, and volunteer cleaning and sanitation services, and he established house rules. The course of history for five thousand people swung a different direction every night on the shoulders of one little man, "the midget with the heart of a giant" as he was known in the East End.[2]

History hinges on human shoulders. People are the bridges others can cross over in their movement toward God's plans for their lives.

THE BARNABAS WAY

If God chooses to direct much of history through people, that means He still wants to do so through you. Every one of us can be a hinge that opens an opportunity for others. And you can be more than that. You can be that supporting structure—the bridge—that others walk across to new chapters in their lives. That's exciting. And our friend Barnabas can show you how.

Barnabas reemerges briefly in just one verse in Acts 9. We haven't heard from him since he put the proceeds from the sale of his land at the apostles' feet back in Acts 4. This one-verse cameo appearance may seem minor or ordinary, but it's not! To catch the significance of it, we're again in need of some context and structure. It's amazing how crucial a role Barnabas plays if you catch a more zoomed-out version of what is occurring when he shows up in that one verse. Here is the small section in which he appears in Acts 9:

> When he [Saul] came to Jerusalem, he tried to join the disciples, but they were all afraid of him, not believing that he really was a disciple. *But Barnabas took him and brought him to the apostles. He told them how Saul on his journey had seen the Lord and that the Lord had spoken to him, and how in Damascus he had preached fearlessly in the name of Jesus.* So Saul stayed with them and moved about freely in Jerusalem, speaking boldly in the name of the Lord. He talked and debated with the Hellenistic Jews, but they tried to kill him. When the believers learned of this, they took him down to Caesarea and sent him off to Tarsus. (Acts 9:26–30, emphasis added)

Barnabas reemerges in this small section in the context of one of the most famous incidents in all of Christian history. No exaggeration! Acts 9 records the conversion of the persecutor-turned-preacher of the church: the apostle Paul (known before his conversion as Saul). It was his Damascus Road conversion, which is so significant an event that the phrase "a Damascus Road experience" is used in contemporary English even today.

It's an idiom for being enlightened. In the book of Acts, this event is so important that the account is repeated three times in detail (also chapters 22 and 26). And who could deny the remarkable stamp of Paul on the Christian church? That all starts here. And while Barnabas makes a tiny, walk-on appearance as a next-to-nobody type of guy—just one verse—this is no insignificant role.

In the broader flow of the book of Acts, the gospel is spreading out of Jerusalem despite opposition toward the ends of the earth through Judea and Samaria. Salvation is available because of what Jesus did in Jerusalem. It was offered to all people as the gospel message began to spread beyond Jerusalem (Acts 1:8). Acts 9:1–30 pauses to focus on Christ's choice servant in this plan: Paul. The broader scene itself has three sections:

- The conversion and call of Paul (9:1–19a)
- The acceptance and rejection of Paul in Damascus (9:19b–25)
- The acceptance and rejection of Paul in Jerusalem (9:26–30)

Lots of irony is involved as God worked in Paul's life here. If ever there was an example of God using *anyone* to accomplish His purposes, it is this one. A complete U-turn was brought about by the grace of God. Without intending any disrespect, this astounding reversal given Paul's murderous hatred for Christians would be like the conversion of Adolf Hitler to orthodox Judaism or Osama bin Laden to US citizenship. Staggering. One who hated a group now joined that group! But note the second and third sections. They are both dealing with the same issue, just in different towns. They are intentionally similar. Barnabas emerged in this third section where Paul was eventually accepted by the church and was rejected by the people of Jerusalem because he preached the gospel.

Now, look specifically at how this third section unfolds structurally in Acts 9:26–30. That alone shows you how crucial Barnabas's role was.

1. Paul tried to join the Jerusalem church (9:26a)
2. The Jerusalem church rejected Paul (9:26b)
3. Barnabas received and spoke up for Paul (9:27)
4. Paul joined the Jerusalem church (9:28–30)
    i. Paul was received (9:28a)
    ii. Paul ministered boldly in Jerusalem (9:28b–29a)
    iii. There was a plot to murder Paul (9:29b)
    iv. The church helped Paul escape to Tarsus (9:30)

Paul tried to join the main church but was rejected. It was only because Barnabas intervened that Paul was received. Barnabas was presented as the hinge that opened up the doorway of Paul's acceptance for fellowship in the Christian church. But Barnabas was also the bridge Paul walked across into official Christian ministry in Jerusalem.

That's the context and structure. It is fascinating. Let's unpack some more details emerging from these verses as we explore two more principles Barnabas modeled for everyday Christians like him to adopt.

The Barnabas Way Is Discerning of Potential in People

Discernment is that ability to perceive and grasp the true nature of what is really going on before it is obvious to others. It is a specific type of sight that peers behind events, situations, decisions, and people and looks into the mechanics that guide them and tracks their trajectories. It grants the ability to make good judgment calls. A discerning person can comprehend what seems obscure to most. She or he can sift wisely between alternatives and then make good choices.

. . . .

BARNABAS PRINCIPLE #4:
DISCERNMENT

A godly influencer detects potential in others.

. . . .

We learn to discern early on. When my son James was just two, he viewed everyone in the world through his own discerning grid. It was a simple question, but you better get it right. Whether we were out and about at the store or church or even at home with guests visiting, he processed everyone through this lens: "Are you a good guy or bad guy?" It was his way of making a judgment call.

If you said, "I'm a good guy," he smiled and gave you the thumbs-up. He approved, and off he went to patrol the next room like the sheriff in an old western. If you said, "I'm a bad guy," his fists would clench and he'd attack, head first. Of course, it was always fun to tell him you are a bad guy just to enjoy his attack. It was even more fun, however, to point at someone else in the room and say, "Hey James, that's a bad guy!" Then you could sit back and enjoy the show. My point is that we learn to discern early on, but it takes some maturity and experience in life to get it right.

Barnabas was a discerning man. He detected the potential in Paul long before anyone else. He discerned that God had a vision for the life of this unusual convert—just as He has for everyone. Barnabas believed bad guys could become good guys if God got ahold of their lives.

Barnabas discerned God's doings in the unusual details occurring around him. He looked carefully at strange events and saw God at work. Barnabas knew that it was Paul who oversaw the execution of his fellow believer Stephen (Acts 8:1). Barnabas was a part of the church in Jerusalem that Paul was destroying as he went from house to house and dragged men and women out to prison (Acts 8:3). In light of what happened to Stephen, the assumption would be that they'd face the same fate too: death by stoning. Barnabas heard Paul's murderous threats in Jerusalem against Christians (Acts 9:1). He knew of Paul's commission by the High Priest to go destroy Christians in Damascus (Acts 9:2). Paul's plans against the church were not private. He was an international assassin, the up-and-coming executioner of Christians to the ends of the earth.

And now this man, Paul, was knocking on the door of the Jerusalem church. He wanted in, not to persecute but rather to preach to all—to the ends of the earth! Something very unusual was going on here, and Barnabas was discerning enough to decipher that these events could be explained only if they were God at work. He had been tracking God's trajectories. He knew God works in the twists and turns of life's daily events. God maneuvers from behind the front stage of life. The incidents may be strange or even coincidental to us, but to a discerning person, these are the subtle workings of the providential hand of God.

Once again, this reminds me of my dad. He is a discerning man who trusts God's providential hand. He daily watches for the Holy Spirit to show up and lead his affairs—to lead him to a situation, to lead him to a conversation. Dad's mindset is to see delays and detours as God's timely rearrangements so that he meets whoever God wants him to meet that day. Every morning just before Dad climbs out of bed, he raises his hands and says a simple prayer: "God, guide me to who You want me to meet for You today." That's a person who looks for God's hand at work in the routine—even unusual—affairs of daily life. And that was Barnabas's approach. God is always up to something. He was up to something in Paul's life.

Barnabas discerned potential when everyone else saw a problem. Barnabas listened attentively to the details of Paul's conversion. He saw God at work in this dubious person. He knew God can do anything with any life, even this one. We don't know when Barnabas got the report that this brutal persecutor was knocking on the door claiming that he now believed Jesus Christ is Lord. But at some point, he looked into it. He did his homework. He listened to the report from Paul, presumably sitting at some form of an ancient coffee shop. That's how he could report to the apostles how Paul had seen the Lord on the road, how the Lord had spoken to him, and how Paul had spoken boldly in the name of Jesus. That's quite a lot of detail that Barnabas knew.

You see, a godly influencer detects potential in others, just as Barnabas did. But once God's work is discerned in a life, there is a next step: risk.

The Barnabas Way Is Risky

Risk is being exposed to some sort of hazard or danger. It increases the likelihood of loss or harm. It brings uncertainty about the future. It's why I hate skydiving and roller coasters. You're supposed to! They just don't seem safe. Risk comes in many forms, including people. People aren't always safe. They can disappoint you, damage you, and destroy you.

BARNABAS PRINCIPLE #5:
RISK

A godly influencer takes risks, and people are always risky!

People are very risky. Certainly, people like Paul are risky. He was a high-risk factor for the church. Yet Barnabas took a big risk on him. It wasn't that Barnabas was a daredevil. Rather, Barnabas was in lockstep with God.

Barnabas led others past Paul's risky past. It was Barnabas who went and found Paul and brought him to the apostles.

He made the introduction and mediated the encounter. The Christian community had already slammed the door shut on Paul. That makes sense to me. I can hear the apostle Peter saying to the apostle John, "Sorry, I must have heard you incorrectly, Brother John. *Who* is knocking at the door? Saul of Tarsus? The chap hunting us down! Are you crazy? Of course he can't come in. Run!" They knew Paul. And they loved Stephen, whose body was still warm in the grave. What if this was a trick? What if this was an attempt to infiltrate the leadership of the church and destroy it from within? I understand slamming the door shut on Paul. He was too risky!

But Barnabas saw past Paul's failed past. He took a risk on someone with an awful track record. But this is classic Barnabas. He looked and discerned God at work in life's strange details. He listened to the account of God's work in this unlikeliest of converts. And then he spoke up for Paul. Barnabas became Paul's advocate. He was a voice for one who did not have—or deserve—a voice. That took courage. Even persecutors of God have opportunities with God. Barnabas believed that. The gospel of Jesus Christ can grab anyone: that neighbor, that family member, that work colleague. Anyone!

Barnabas bridged Paul's potential toward ministry. We don't get the details about how the apostles deliberated Barnabas's report. They just trusted him. We're simply told in verses 28–30 that Paul joined the group and ministered in Jerusalem so boldly that there was a murder plot on his life and he needed to escape. But don't ignore the fact that the shift in Paul's trajectory in church fellowship and Christian ministry is because of verse 27. It's because of Barnabas's relationship and reputation with those who nicknamed him "son of encouragement" that Paul got an audience and acceptance.

A beautiful irony occurs here that is a testimony to the grace of God, the type of redemptive reversal that Barnabas discerned God could be doing. We are told that Paul was talking and debating with the Hellenists, but they were trying to kill him. This is likely the same Hellenistic group in Jerusalem that Stephen was so effective in debating and that had plotted to murder him some time back (Acts 6:9–15). It was murder under Paul's supervision. We are to make the ironic connection. Paul went into a lion's den in which he once stood as king of the beasts. What a redemptive twist!

THE BARNABAS WAY THROUGH YOU

God's view of every life is potential, not past. It's always future-oriented. It looks at what could be, not what was. Anyone can become anything despite any circumstance *if* in God's hands. Barnabas believed that. He discerned the workings of the gospel in unusual incidents and in unlikely people. And so he positioned himself alongside Paul, using his clout to reconcile enemies and launch another gospel servant. Barnabas had a vision for Paul's life simply because God did. And Barnabas used his networking credit to get Paul moving. God, of course, could have used someone else to launch Paul. But Barnabas was that ordinary believer who was available and willing.

And so the question for you is, Are you available and willing? Will you choose to see those around you the way God does, as brimming with potential despite their obvious failures? It's amazing what could be unleashed in the life of another simply through your kind words, listening ears, helping hands, and connections. And that is what God wants from you. He wants to use you today to change the trajectory of someone else's life. He still works through available and willing people. But you are forewarned: influencing people for Christ is risky, and track records are hard to ignore. This is no easy task, but it's worth it. In seeing beyond people's pasts, you, too, can live out what Jesus taught us to pray: "Forgive us our sins, for we also forgive everyone who sins against us" (Luke 11:4). You can live out the truth that God forgave you in Christ. All of us are like the proverbial turtle sitting on top of a fence post. It didn't get there alone. Someone lifted it up! And we didn't get where we are on our own. Risking on people is lifting others where they couldn't get to on their own. It is a heavenly investment. In that case, risk is just another word for faith. Risk—with God involved—is faith.

As a hinge and a bridge, Barnabas displayed interpersonal intelligence: the ability to grasp and interact effectively with others sensitive to varying perspectives.[3] Like him, you can develop those necessary people skills. You must look at the circumstances around you and watch where God shows up. There are no coincidences, just God-given opportunities. You must listen to what is going on around you in the culture to detect God's redemptive stories unfolding. They are unbelievable!

You must speak up to lead others beyond their risks, failures, and disappointments. There is potential to fulfill in every life. Finally, you must launch others (not yourself) using your God-given resources.

Look. Listen. Speak up. Launch. You can do that today for someone. You are to be a hinge to open doors of opportunities for others. You can be a bridge for others to cross in their walk with God.

Some Food for Thought

IN ORDER TO BENEFIT MOST FROM THE TRUTHS IN this chapter, think through each major section and then answer the following questions:

1. Think of those people in your past who invested in you. What did they do? Do they know the role they played?

2. People are risky. We all are. But to influence people we must be quick to forgive their failures. Meditate on Jesus' words on forgiveness in Luke 11:4. Reflect on all that He forgave you.

3. Barnabas discerned God's hand at work in those around him. He also displayed interpersonal intelligence. If you are a ministry leader in any capacity, what relationships around you need to be connected or reconciled? How could you mediate this?

CHAPTER 4

Pickers and Piggybackers

Launching Others Without Competing

I will build my church.
JESUS

The best executive is the one who has enough sense to pick good men to do what he wants done, and self-restraint enough to keep from meddling with others while they do it.
PRESIDENT TEDDY ROOSEVELT

ON MAY 4, 1904, A REMARKABLE MEETING OCCURRED at the Midland Hotel in Manchester, England, when two men who had never met sat across from each other. Only one of the two was genuinely interested in a conversation. The men had little in common, and the differences between them were enormous by the social standards of the day.

Seated on one side was Henry. He was forty-one years old and from a poor, working-class background. He was the youngest of five children and his father had died when he was around nine. This meant that Henry was out at work delivering telegrams and selling newspapers on the streets at a young age. He received very limited schooling (a year or so) and hopped from job to job as the years unfolded, trying to scrape a living. He eventually started a small business.

Across from Henry sat Charles. He was twenty-six years old and from the upper classes of society—the son of the 1st Baron Llangattock. That's right, he was a member of the nobility. Charles was born into privilege at a time when society was structured with just a few at the top and everyone else at the bottom. (Think *Downton Abbey* if that means anything to you.) He enjoyed the comforts and opportunities his lineage gave him. He was educated right through to the university level at Trinity College, Cambridge. He was set up for a successful business with great networks by his dad. And he enjoyed the time and financial freedom to play and sport where he chose. His was a luxurious life.

And now these two sat across from each other at the hotel. Charles (the nobleman) had called the meeting and traveled to Henry, such was his interest. Henry was simply being courteous given the effort Charles had made traveling up from London. As different as these two men were, they both shared one core passion. They were what we would today call *techies*; they were enthusiasts of the latest technology. In 1904, this wasn't mobile phones and computer tablets—it was motor cars. Car talk was the reason for this gathering.

Henry's hopping from one job to another from youth had exposed him to engineering. It had become his passion, particularly motor engineering. He'd set up a company, bought a used French car, dismantled it, and built a better one. He repeated this a few times, and one of these rebuilds made its way to Charles. Charles was also passionate about motor cars and marketing. His father had set him up in a dealership importing foreign cars. But Charles knew that nothing he imported came close to the quality of what Henry built.

And so the purpose of this meeting in Manchester was to tap into a mutual passion: to build the best car in the world. Charles picked the best engineer on the planet, Henry, who in turn piggybacked off Charles's business networks and marketing expertise. The result of this gathering between Charles

Rolls and Henry Royce was the birth of the best car in the world: the Rolls-Royce.

And the result was not just the best cars in the world but (in the other new techie industry at the time) the best airplanes! Rolls-Royce took off from there as the twentieth century unfolded. By 1987, Rolls-Royce was second only to Coca-Cola in brand recognition across the world.[1] And what was a key reason for this success from the start? Partnership. Teamwork. Collaboration. Charles and Henry picked the right partners to work with and piggybacked off each other's separate skill sets to achieve that mutual passion: building the best car in the world.

HOW TO REACH GOD-GIVEN POTENTIAL

Selecting key people around you and giving them a foothold toward success in light of their talents is essential to any successful group endeavor. The Great Commission is a group endeavor. All followers of Jesus Christ must work selflessly as a team in our mutual passion: not to build the best engine in the world but to spread the best news across the world. We are joining Jesus as He builds His church.

One of my favorite books in the area of influencing others and pursuing a group goal is a small leadership book by Max De Pree entitled *Leadership Is an Art*. Clearly, I'm not the only one who appreciated what De Pree said. The book has sold close to a million copies! One of the key reasons I like it so much is because I see in De Pree's advice to the corporate world his clear Christian convictions. De Pree was not just an extremely successful business leader and author; he was a committed follower of Jesus Christ. Christian principles work their way out in the book. Clearest of all is the basic scriptural belief that there is potential in the people around you. Those around you have not only sacred worth but staggering, God-given potential. It just needs drawing out. De Pree wrote, "Three of the key elements in the art of working together are how to deal with change, how to deal with conflict, *and how to reach our potential.*"[2]

De Pree was right. People around us have potential. They have a helpful voice—listen. They are gifted—use them. They add to the task at hand—partner with them. Team up and collaborate with those God has placed beside you. This participative approach that De Pree called for in the business world is essential in the church's mission of spreading the gospel across the entire world. It's the same teamwork Henry Royce and Charles Rolls understood. It's what the Scriptures mean by calling the church a body or a building—diverse pieces coming together as one.[3]

All that to say, those around you are talented. At times they may not look like it, dress like it, or act like it, but they really are! Their potential needs to be drawn out, engaged, and released. They need to be picked out for godly use and then piggybacked toward success—that is, toward God's plan for their lives. That's the good life; that's success.

THE BARNABAS WAY

Barnabas was a picker and a piggybacker. He got those around him involved. He made sure he gave them the lift they needed to succeed as God intended. We see this clearly as his role in the book of Acts begins to increase and he is used by God to lead the first globally minded church in history, the church in the city of Antioch.

Up until this point in Acts, we've seen Barnabas emerge gradually through a few verses in Acts 4 and one in Acts 9. But in Acts 11 God begins to shine the spotlight on him some more in the pages of Scripture. God wants us to see His choice role model as the leader of the first church that strategically planned to spread the gospel to the ends of the earth.

Now those who had been scattered by the persecution that broke out when Stephen was killed traveled as far as Phoenicia, Cyprus and Antioch, spreading the word only among Jews. Some of them, however, men from Cyprus and Cyrene, went to Antioch and began to speak to Greeks also, telling them the good news about the Lord Jesus. The Lord's hand was with them, and a great number of people believed and turned to the Lord.

News of this reached the church in Jerusalem, and they sent Barnabas to Antioch. When he arrived and saw what the grace of God had done, he was glad and encouraged them all to remain true to the Lord with all their hearts.

He was a good man, full of the Holy Spirit and faith, and a great number of people were brought to the Lord.

Then Barnabas went to Tarsus to look for Saul, and when he found him, he brought him to Antioch. So for a whole year Barnabas and Saul met with the church and taught great numbers of people. The disciples were called Christians first at Antioch.

During this time some prophets came down from Jerusalem to Antioch. One of them, named Agabus, stood up and through the Spirit predicted that a severe famine would spread over the entire Roman world. (This happened during the reign of Claudius.) The disciples, as each one was able, decided to provide help for the brothers and sisters living in Judea. This they did, sending their gift to the elders by Barnabas and Saul. (Acts 11:19–30)

When we left Barnabas in that cameo appearance back in Acts 9:27, he was the human hinge that swung open the door for Paul's acceptance into the church. Furthermore, he was the human bridge Paul walked across toward ministry life. Much has happened since then in the book of Acts. If you recall, Acts is the record of the activities of the Holy Spirit through followers of Jesus. Acts tells the story of the unfolding of Jesus' words in Acts 1:8 that His followers bear witness to Him, beginning in Jerusalem and extending to the far reaches of the world—all in the power of the Holy Spirit. And this was occurring.

The book of Acts captures this flow in its broad structure. In its introduction (1:1–11), we read Jesus' final instructions to His disciples, just before He was taken up to heaven: "and you will be my witnesses in Jerusalem, and in all Judea and Samaria, and to the ends of the earth" (v. 8). Then the rest of the book of Acts shows Jesus' followers carrying out that mission:

1. Witnesses of Jesus throughout *Jerusalem* (1:12–8:3)
2. Witnesses of Jesus throughout *Judea and Samaria* (8:4–11:18)
3. Witnesses of Jesus throughout the *ends of the earth* (11:19–28:31)

What I want you to see is that this next account of Barnabas launches the third major section of that flow of Acts—the spread of the gospel of Jesus Christ to the ends of the earth. Barnabas was key right at the beginning of this global move.

Barnabas was chosen by God to play a crucial role in the establishment of that first church that actively implemented God's vision to take the gospel to all. Again, our passage makes it clear that the hand of God was driving this move (11:21). These are the activities of the Holy Spirit! Sometimes He uses persecution or hardship to accomplish His purposes (vv. 19–20), but He also uses regular people like Barnabas and you and me.

Antioch was a great city in Syria from which to launch this third move. As the third-largest city in the world at that time (after Rome and Alexandria), it was a very important part of the Roman world.[4] It was diverse and prosperous. It was strategically placed for global travel and trade since it was close to the sea, beside a big river, and on the major trade routes.

It is no surprise that God picked this place to plant a globally focused church to fulfill His mission. Nor is it surprising that He picked Barnabas to lead that first global outreach. God's pick, Barnabas, modeled two more principles for everyday Christians to copy.

The Barnabas Way Guides Others

An authentic influencer leads regardless of any formal position of leadership. We've already seen that Barnabas influenced those around him from wherever God placed him. Up to this point it's not been from an official leadership role. We, too, must lead whoever is nearby from whatever position God has us in, even if it means stepping into formal leadership roles from time to time. Several insights emerge from Barnabas's willingness to step up into a more formal leadership role.

. . . .

BARNABAS PRINCIPLE #6:
LEAD

A godly influencer leads.

. . . .

Barnabas was picked to lead and bring organization to the task at hand. Barnabas emerges in Acts 11 as a sort of senior pastor in the church at Antioch. He brought order and direction to this new church plant, the effects of which we will see in our next chapter. Barnabas was specifically picked to do this, which again reveals his reputation among the leaders of the church in Jerusalem.

They didn't send just anyone up to Antioch; they chose someone who could administrate and pastor people. In fact, previously in Acts 8, the leadership sent none other than the apostles Peter and John up to Samaria to assess and organize the spread of the gospel into the second phase of God's plan: the witness of the gospel in Judea and Samaria (8:4–11:18). As we enter this third movement, they picked Barnabas. That's a massive vote of confidence in Barnabas's leadership and organizational skills.

Barnabas was chosen and so he steps up. He didn't shrink back. Upon arrival, he took note of what was happening. He discerned it to be the work of God. He rejoiced with the believers and encouraged them to live with devotion to God. He also became their teacher, a role in Acts so far that was associated with the apostles as leaders of the church. Barnabas established this church plant into a healthy and outward-looking body. He moved them in the right direction; he led them to catch God's vision for the world, which we see unfold a few chapters later.

Barnabas was a leader qualified by godly character. A key qualification in the Scriptures for a godly influencer—be it a servant leader in a ministry or an everyday believer wanting to shape those around them—is godly character. When character, competence, and convictions merge in an individual, you have the makings of an authentic influencer. Skill sets and know-how (competence) and a commitment to truth with passion and vision (convictions) will collapse if the person does not have moral qualities and integrity (character)—*godly* character. It is indispensable.

Influence, at whatever level, is godly only if the heart is transformed to follow the pattern of Jesus Christ and produces the fruit of the Spirit. God wants us to know that Barnabas's qualification to represent Him in this pastoral role was in his heart: "He was a good man, full of the Holy Spirit and faith" (Acts 11:24).

Barnabas was a generous leader who led a church to generosity. When we were introduced to Barnabas in Acts 4, he was a role model of generosity to those around him; he was sacrificial in his giving. This emerges again. While it is mentioned briefly, it is significant. God sent word through a prophet concerning a famine that was about to occur, and those whom Barnabas had taught to discern God's Word responded with a relief mission. They set up a benevolence fund. The outward and self-sacrificial generosity of the believers at Antioch is but one expression of what they'd been taught from their leader. Barnabas had been their teacher for a year, and as we've seen, he showed God's people how to be generous. He was contagious!

The Barnabas Way Enlists Others

Barnabas wasn't just picked to head up affairs in Antioch for a season. He also picked people around him and gave them a piggyback in ministry. A good leader does that; everyday influencers shape others by getting them involved. They delegate well. As President Theodore Roosevelt is widely reported to have said, "The best executive is the one who has enough sense to pick good men to do what he wants done, and self-restraint enough to keep from meddling with others while they do it." Barnabas led well and delegated wisely.

Barnabas delegated through team ministry. Part of bringing order to the new church in Antioch involved meeting its practical needs. These new believers needed encouragement. They needed to be taught. They needed to mobilize so they could reach out.

....

BARNABAS PRINCIPLE #7: *DELEGATE*

A godly influencer delegates but doesn't compete.

....

But Barnabas realized he couldn't do it alone. Doing it alone would stifle the potential in Antioch. So Barnabas left Antioch and made his way to Tarsus for a short trip. He went there to find Paul, who had been doing who knows what since we left him in Acts 9. Barnabas brought him to Antioch because he knew Paul could help.

This is because Barnabas believed in team ministry. He was living out what leadership experts recommend today. Our friend Max De Pree wrote,

> In addition to all of the ratios and goals and parameters
> and bottom lines, it is fundamental that leaders endorse
> a concept of persons. This begins with an understand-
> ing of the diversity of people's gifts and talents and skills.
> Understanding and accepting diversity enables us to see
> that each of us is needed. It also enables us to begin to think

about being abandoned to the strengths of others, of admitting that we cannot *know* or *do* everything.[5]

Barnabas believed the church in Antioch would thrive all the more if others were involved. And now, with the help of Paul and for an entire year, they "met with the church and taught great numbers of people" (Acts 11:26). What a blessing!

And what risk! Remember, this church was founded by "those who had been scattered by the persecution that broke out when Stephen was killed" (11:19). That is another way of saying that this church was started by those who were chased by Paul's murderous threats. Can you imagine the response in that church when Barnabas came back from his trip with Paul by his side? It is a little like what the apostles would have thought in Jerusalem in Acts 9. These people lost loved ones because of Paul, and now he was there to minister and teach. Seriously, Barnabas? But Barnabas, true to form, took a risk *again* on a risky person because he was a team player and knew precisely who Antioch needed. Because of Barnabas's reputation, presence, and supervision, Paul joined the fellowship in Antioch and also ministered among them.

All that to say, Barnabas did for Paul in Antioch what he did for Paul in Jerusalem. He was a hinge to fellowship and a bridge to new areas of ministry. He took risks on risky people.

Barnabas didn't see Paul as a threat to stifle but as a talent to launch. Barnabas picked Paul in order to piggyback him to global ministry. Barnabas was well aware of the potential in this ordinary Christian man sitting at home in Tarsus twiddling his thumbs, waiting for God to use him. And Barnabas didn't perceive Paul's gifts as a threat to his own ministry success. What if Paul was a better teacher? What if Paul went beyond where Barnabas ever went in ministry impact? These were not issues of concern for Barnabas because (remember) he was a godly man—"a good man, full of the Holy Spirit and faith" (Acts 11:24). Godly people don't lose sleep over issues of popularity.

I've been around ministry long enough to see that dangerous ego we talked about in chapter 1. Do you remember? That pitfall of one's own inflated sense of self-importance can drive any of us to all sorts of sins, including selfish ambition. It can manifest itself in characterizing one's desire to grow a personal ministry and reputation as a desire to be "fruitful for God's glory." Don't get me wrong. I want fruitful ministries. I'm just saying that I question the motivation behind some I've observed. If you strip away some of the humble mumbo jumbo, you see that too many perceive even ministry as a competition or personal launchpad—a bigger church, more followers on social media, a better-known name, making it on some sort of "success" list, and so on. It's quite self-promoting. It's as though the world's measurement of success—bigger, better, more—is God's measurement of success. It's not! All God is interested in is faithfulness.

My parents' ministry in Spain, for example, over nearly four decades was a success despite the low numbers at church; it was a success because they were faithful. That's it. Nothing more. Nothing to add up or measure there. No comparison with someone else's calling. Perhaps the only tangible metric were ministry scars. Numbers as "fruit of ministry" are up to God; He causes the growth. We're simply to be faithful.

But how we *view* ministry impacts how we *do* ministry. If we view ministry with an eye toward our own success, then we do ministry to that end. I read of an interesting social experiment.[6] It concerned the observation of two sets of groups playing the same game. The first group was told it was a *community* game. The second group was told the game was a *Wall Street* game. Although both groups were playing the exact same game, the way it unfolded was strikingly different. When the game was deemed a community engagement, participants cooperated and helped each other along. In the one labeled a Wall Street game, they competed aggressively against each other. The name of the game affected the way it was played.

For Barnabas, the name of the game was advancing Jesus. That's it! This meant team ministry. This meant partnering with and promoting others noncompetitively. Barnabas did not see the potential gifts and success of another believer as a threat to him. He didn't care who got the credit, more recognition, and thousands of "likes" on social media. All that mattered to him was Jesus. That's the one "like" you want to receive on the day you stand before Him! And so, with that mindset, Barnabas went and picked Saul off the couch in Tarsus, piggybacked him to his first pulpit in Antioch, and gave us the apostle Paul!

THE BARNABAS WAY THROUGH YOU

Barnabas picked without prying and piggybacked others without competing. That's remarkable self-restraint, humility, and godly self-confidence. We see this in his leadership of the first globally minded church that caught God's vision for the world and executed it in action through missions.

It is no coincidence that God chose Barnabas for that role. He possessed the organizational intelligence necessary—that is, the ability to understand a group, organize it efficiently, and direct its mission. He brought this skill to the church of Antioch. And what about the irony of it all? A church planted because of Paul's persecution became the church that spread the gospel to the ends of the earth through Paul's preaching. Only God can orchestrate that reversal. And Barnabas was His key player.

One of the (many) remarkable traits of Barnabas—seen here and in all the places he pops up—is his unquestioned versatility. He was willing to take on any role. He was a giver, an advocate, a representative, and a ministry leader, and there was more to come. He slipped into whatever role God asked him to take. Barnabas was like the well-known story of the two angels. It is often attributed to the former slave trader who became the hymn writer of *Amazing Grace*, John Newton. But we don't really know where it came from. It declares,

> If two angels were to receive at the same moment a commission from God, one to go down and rule earth's grandest

empire, the other to go and sweep the streets of its meanest village, it would be a matter of entire indifference to each which service fell to his lot, the post of ruler or the post of scavenger; for the joy of the angels lies only in obedience to God's will, and with equal joy, they would lift a Lazarus in his rags to Abraham's bosom, or be a chariot of fire to carry an Elijah home.

Like these angels, Barnabas was happy to be obedient. He stepped up to lead. He was happy to delegate. He was a picker of "nobodies" with potential and a piggybacker who carried them toward God's vision for their lives. Barnabas found the potential in people and then made sure he launched it.

And so, once again, the questions for you are many and challenging. Are you willing to step up to formal leadership if need be? Are you willing to step down from formal leadership to delegate and launch others to godly success beyond you? Are your eyes open to pick people around you and launch their potential past you? Are you even willing to be the one who piggybacks them to success past yours? These are convicting questions. To all of them, Barnabas answered yes! And Barnabas is our God-given role model.

Some Food for Thought

ONCE AGAIN, IT IS IMPORTANT TO THINK YOUR WAY through the major sections in this chapter before attempting to answer the following questions:

1. The Great Commission is a personal and communal call. Partnership is efficient and fulfilling. Together we really are better! Take a look at 1 Corinthians 12:12–26 and Ephesians 2:21–22. How can you collaborate with other Christians in making disciples?

2. Picking without prying. Piggybacking without competing. What do these phrases mean to you?

3. The foundational qualification for ministry leadership is a godly heart. But leadership also requires organizational intelligence. Revisit Acts 11:19–30 with an eye on those issues Barnabas engaged in to establish and lead this church.

CHAPTER 5

Plodders and Mentors

The Value of Meaningful Presence

The harvest is plentiful but the workers are few.
JESUS

God, give me Scotland or I die.
JOHN KNOX

WILLIAM CAREY IS KNOWN AS THE FATHER OF MOD-
ern Christian missions. It's perhaps a bit of an exaggeration to
give anyone that label, but there is no doubt the shoemaker-
turned-missionary was a role model of service to the Lord
Jesus Christ across the world.

While fixing shoes in England in the eighteenth century,
he caught God's vision for reaching the world with the gospel of Jesus Christ. He then packed his bags in England and
went to India. Carey was there for forty-one years without ever
returning home. His ministry was filled with difficulty and
pain, including the loss of many loved ones along the way. But
his impact for Christ was huge because he persevered in God's
call on his life.

The results of Carey's influence are still felt in India today:
in education, in the founding of many churches, in establishing
the Baptist Missionary Society, and even in horticulture.
Perhaps most significant was his work in the translation of the
Bible into many languages like Bengali, Hindi, and Marathi.
Those are the primary languages of around 635 million people
today scattered across India, Bangladesh, Pakistan, and even
the United States and the United Kingdom. Christian philo-
sopher and Indian author Vishal Mangalwadi captured Carey's

influence beautifully when he stated that Carey "saw India not as a foreign country to be exploited, but as the heavenly Father's land to be loved."[1]

Carey loved God and people. This expressed itself in active service to Christ. His own words challenge any follower of Jesus today. He said, "If after my death anyone should think it worthwhile to write of my life, I will give you a criterion by which you may judge its accuracy. If he gives me credit for being a plodder, he will describe me accurately. Anything beyond this will be too much. I can plod."[2] William Carey was a plodder. Nothing more and nothing less. That's the label he gave himself: He was not the father of modern missions but a plodder for Jesus Christ. Carey simply stuck it out at God's call!

For many years I studied in Edinburgh, Scotland. It is a beautiful city with a rich and troubled history. It really is worth adding to your bucket list! God grabbed my heart there during those college years in remarkable ways, including one visit to the little town of St. Andrews just up the coast. If you ever get to visit this great land, go to St. Andrews. There is an interesting feature on some roads: initials. There is PH, which stands for Patrick Hamilton. To this day, it is a tradition for students at the university to hop over the letters, fearing they'll fail their exams if they step on them. Patrick Hamilton was burned at the stake for preaching the gospel of Jesus Christ. He was only twenty-five years old. And then there are the initials GW popping out in stone on the asphalt road. These refer to George Wishart. Like Carey, he was a steady plodder for Jesus too.

Wishart was a man who walked across Scotland in the sixteenth century preaching God's truth and was under constant threat. Such was the danger to his life that he had a pupil-turned-bodyguard stand behind him with a sword for protection as he preached. George ultimately was burned publicly for his preaching. And on his way to death, he told his bodyguard to stand down with the sword and step up in the call to preach the gospel across the land. It was now his turn! As Wishart's bones burned to cinders, the bodyguard determined to bring Scotland to its knees in faith to Jesus Christ. And this he did. The apprentice and bodyguard mentored by George Wishart was none other than the famous Scottish reformer John Knox. His prayers were feared more than all the gathered armies of Europe, and his own prayer motto in life was, "God, give me Scotland or I die!"

William Carey. George Wishart. John Knox. Everyday men who became remarkable followers of Jesus Christ. I confess I have a soft spot for missionaries and preaching pastors given my background. Like these men, they're plodders. They press on through thick and thin. They persevere. They keep going despite the circumstances, discouragement, little appreciation, and often tight family budgets—very tight! I know this well. I grew up in a missionary-pastor home. Yet, like Wishart, they pour out their lives to spread the gospel, shepherd souls, and mentor others like John Knox to influence the world.

Missionaries and pastors are heroes! They preach. They pastor. They mentor. They plod.

"THIS JEWEL AMONG HOBBITS"

Plodders. Mentors. It's what each follower of Jesus should aspire to become. Men and women who persevere in the call of the Great Commission, come what may. Men and women who coach and develop whoever is around them so that they will live for Jesus Christ. After all, the Great Commission is about forming people through thick and thin; it means coming alongside others and mentoring them in obedience to the Lord Jesus Christ.

A striking, and now global, illustration of an ever-present plodder who mentors a friend to success comes to us through fiction from the pen of J. R. R. Tolkien. While the novel *The Lord of the Rings* is fantasy, its author was a committed Christian. Much like C. S. Lewis, Tolkien (who led Lewis to faith in Jesus Christ) inserted scriptural truths within his fictional works.

The Lord of the Rings is set in an imaginary war between good and evil. But it is a reflection of the real history of World War I, in which Tolkien served as an officer. It was a brutal war. This "war to end all wars" left more boys dead in muddy ditches and mustard gas–polluted puddles than any other. Europe was plowed like a farmer's field by bombs!

The main character in the story is called Frodo, and he's a

hobbit. Now, hobbits by Tolkien's literary design are not supposed to be picked as world changers, never mind world savers.
They are small, weak, jolly, and insignificant humanlike creatures in Tolkien's make-believe world. They are "nobodies"!
But they are also courageous, loyal, selfless, and determined.
While Frodo gets attention for saving that world from evil, he
is able to do so only because of the loyal, selfless, and dogged
presence of his buddy, Samwise Gamgee. He coaches Frodo
along. He sticks to Frodo's side all the way. He plods along with
Frodo on the mission when all seems lost.

That isn't my subjective interpretation of the story. It's
Tolkien's own opinion. For Tolkien, Gamgee was the reflection
of the ordinary, low-ranking soldier selflessly and sacrificially
serving under him in World War I. In a war that butchered
over six thousand soldiers like these *per day* for *four years*,
Tolkien observed, "My 'Sam Gamgee' is indeed a reflection of
the English soldier, of the privates and batmen I knew in the
1914 war, and recognized as so far superior to myself."[3] That's
why he made the hobbits the heroes of *The Lord of the Rings*.
Hobbits are the fictional depiction of the ordinary, unassum-
ing soldiers who fought in the war. And chief among the heroes
for Tolkien in his story is not Frodo but Samwise Gamgee,
whom he called "this jewel among hobbits."[4]

Few followers of Jesus Christ serve in the public eye or as
major protagonists in God's story of Scripture. None of us are
generals or mighty-looking warriors. And even those who do
catch substantial public attention are just regular followers of
Jesus whom God chose to spotlight. And He did so for some

long after they died. All that to say, whatever notoriety others get belongs to God. And whatever notoriety you do or don't get belongs to God too. Notoriety is not ours to plod for. In the mission to be world changers by proclaiming our Savior, Jesus Christ, we each have a role. That's what we plod at. As each of us plods along faithfully in the spread of the gospel and as we mentor whoever happens to be around us, we influence our culture for Jesus Christ.

THE BARNABAS WAY

Barnabas was a plodder and a mentor. He understood God's vision for the world expressed in the Great Commission. We've seen him living it out in different ways in the book of Acts. And now he models for us what sticking at it and developing others can do. His life shows us how to plod and mentor. We've seen this already, of course, as he enabled Paul's fellowship and ministry in Jerusalem and Antioch. But now we see Barnabas empower Paul in world missions right there beside him; Barnabas is like this jewel among humanity to Paul. The first missionary expedition in the book of Acts is presented in Acts 13–14. Here is the beginning and end of that section:

> Now in the church at Antioch there were prophets and teachers: Barnabas, Simeon called Niger, Lucius of Cyrene, Manaen (who had been brought up with Herod the tetrarch) and Saul. While they were worshiping the Lord and fasting,

the Holy Spirit said, "Set apart for me Barnabas and Saul for the work to which I have called them." So after they had fasted and prayed, they placed their hands on them and sent them off. (Acts 13:1–3)

From Attalia they sailed back to Antioch, where they had been committed to the grace of God for the work they had now completed. On arriving there, they gathered the church together and reported all that God had done through them and how he had opened a door of faith to the Gentiles. And they stayed there a long time with the disciples. (Acts 14:26–28)

At the start of this section we're back in the church of Antioch with Barnabas and Paul after we last saw them heading off on a relief mission with a financial gift to the churches in Judea in Acts 11. In Acts 13, we see they have returned back to Antioch because this is now their home church. And what a church it is becoming under the leadership of Barnabas. Note that he heads the list of leaders (13:1). This was God's strategic church to take the gospel of Jesus Christ to the ends of the earth.

The First International Missionary Expedition

Acts 13–14 records the first official and international missionary expedition by a local church to that end. A general summary of each section of the journey sets us up to see how to follow in the footsteps of our role model.

Introduction in Antioch (13:1–3). The section begins with a list of key leaders in the church in Antioch. The emphasis here is that the Holy Spirit called for this first missionary ministry. This is a record of the acts of the Holy Spirit through the church. It is God's plan that was unfolding. God executes His vision through church missions.

The gospel in Cyprus (13:4–12). The first place Barnabas and Paul visit is the island of Cyprus. It was a prosperous island for many reasons, including its strategic location in the Mediterranean Sea. On this island, the gospel spread despite opposition. The irony is that a Gentile leader, called Sergius Paulos, believed in Jesus, while a Jewish false prophet did not.

The gospel in Pisidian Antioch (13:13–52). The missionary expedition then moved on to a different Antioch (of Pisidia) in what is modern-day Turkey. It, too, was a strategic city because an ancient highway, the Via Sebaste, went through it, funneling all sorts of trade down its streets. The gospel spread here, and many believed despite the verbal abuse and eventual expulsion from the city that Barnabas and Paul experienced. Paul preached in the Jewish church concerning Jesus as the fulfillment of their Hebrew Bible. It is here where young John Mark, Barnabas and Paul's assistant, left them to return to Jerusalem.

The gospel in Iconium (14:1–7). After being ejected from Pisidian Antioch, Barnabas and Paul continued to Iconium, also in what is modern-day Turkey. Little is known of this town other than it also was prosperous and strategic for trade. The missionary party spread the gospel here and, once again, were opposed. This time the opposition escalated with a threat and a plot to stone the missionaries.

The gospel in Lystra (14:8–20). The next stop was a nearby town called Lystra. It was not a major town (more of a backwater place), but God wants to reach all people. This town had a developed cult of worship to the highest god in the Greco-Roman group of gods: Zeus. There was not only a temple to Zeus but also a priesthood to manage his affairs with the locals. And, you guessed it, the gospel spread here as well and was rejected. The rejection intensified from expulsion in Pisidian Antioch to threats of stoning in Iconium and now to actual stoning in Lystra.

Conclusion in Antioch (14:21–28). The final scene in this first missionary journey records the path back to the home church in Antioch, Syria. Barnabas and Paul retraced their steps and established churches. They warned believers of what would happen: hardship. Upon arrival in Antioch, they reported all that God had done in spreading the gospel in Gentile lands.

That is a run-down of the spread of the gospel in this first international missionary expedition. Now, let's look specifically at two more principles that emerge from the life of Barnabas as the party traveled along.

The Barnabas Way Sticks at It to Launch Others

An authentic life of influence is concerned with catapulting others toward God's vision for their lives. That kind of person wants to enable and empower others rather than stifle them. To promote and launch others is not difficult for those secure

in their own role before God. Barnabas was such a man. While he was capable of doing all that we see occurring in this missionary journey, we see him launching Paul forward and often stepping back himself.

. . . .

BARNABAS PRINCIPLE #8:
EMPOWER

A godly influencer launches potential in protégés.

. . . .

Barnabas was the leader, but leaders launch others. While it is true that this was Paul's first international missionary expedition, that does not mean he led the journey. On the contrary, this mission trip was led by Barnabas.

Barnabas is presented in the details of this account as the leader the Holy Spirit called to head up the trip. A few key incidents signal this. His name is listed first among the names given in Acts 13:1. In that world, lists like this with multiple names began with the perceived leader of the group. And, of course, we've already seen in the previous chapter that Barnabas was the leader of the Antioch church. Moreover, in verse 2 we have a direct quote of the voice of the Holy Spirit. He, too, names Barnabas first. Now, while the expedition is primarily referred to as Paul's from Acts 13:13 onward, a significant and revealing point is made later in chapter 14. There, in Lystra, where there was a cult to Zeus, the people believed that Barnabas was Zeus and that Paul was only Zeus's spokesperson, Hermes.

They perceived Barnabas to be the leader of the missionary group—the chief god!

Although Barnabas was the leader of the ministry expedition, he clearly stepped into the background in the key incidents recorded throughout it. He allowed his apprentice, Paul, to develop and express his God-given gifts and calling. Ultimately, Barnabas supervised the increasing role Paul would play in ministry and in the remainder of the book of Acts. In Acts 11 (at the church in Antioch) Barnabas enlisted and engaged Paul in local church ministry. And here we see Barnabas empower Paul in ministry life as they plodded along in missionary activity.

Godly influencers actively launch the potential in protégés.

The Barnabas Way Shapes Others Up Close in Life

As the role of Barnabas in the book of Acts increases, it becomes more evident that his influence was through personal, hands-on involvement. We are back to the discipleship as *imitatio*, which we talked about already. We rub off on one another. Who others become is more caught than taught.

BARNABAS PRINCIPLE #9:
EXAMPLE

A godly influencer develops by example—hands-on!

Barnabas developed others side by side. Barnabas shaped Paul not only in situ (that is, while doing ministry) but also alongside him, life-on-life. He mentored Paul by being meaningfully present. Paul wasn't sent out on his own—not yet. He was sent out by the Holy Spirit *with* Barnabas. That is to say, what we see in this evangelistic ministry is that Barnabas mentored Paul on the mission field just as he did in Acts 11 in local church ministry. In the process of this meaningful relationship, Paul's skills and gifting were manifested and flourished. Barnabas was Paul's mentor. He coached him personally: side by side.

Barnabas was happy to lead and *follow.* In launching and empowering Paul, Barnabas was happy to follow. John Mark was the one who left right when Paul seemed to gain prominence. We don't know why he left the missionary expedition. As you will see later, we do know it was not for good reason, given it upset Paul. But Barnabas was content with Paul taking a leadership role, performing the miracles that proved the message as well as stepping up to preach in the synagogues when asked. As we've seen before, Barnabas did not see someone else's gifts and success as a threat to his own calling by God. He stepped up to lead. He stepped aside to mentor. He stepped back to follow.

Barnabas modeled influence on one's knees. It is clear the senior pastor in the church of Antioch was Barnabas. When we re-encounter him with his ministry team here in Acts 13, we see him leading them in prayer. Prayer and fasting express a desire to hear the voice of God. It is that spiritual discipline that positions one in an environment or mindset that speaks to God, listens for His voice, and expresses humility and neediness to Him. The result here? The Holy Spirit spoke. Their response? They went back to fasting and prayer before they set off to foreign shores to spread the gospel. That's the ministry leadership Barnabas modeled: one saturated in prayer. An authentic life of influence is one regularly on your knees.

Charles Haddon Spurgeon was a great man of God and a pastor-preacher in nineteenth-century London. Such was his gift of preaching and impact on his generation that he is still known as the prince of preachers. God used him to reach millions with the gospel of Jesus Christ. Spurgeon credited this to the work of God in response to the prayers of the people of God. When asked why so many were coming to faith, he often pointed to the hundreds who gathered to intercede for souls before church services. If one visited his church and ran into him, he was known to take visitors to the basement prayer room and point them to those there on their knees before God and tell them, "Here is the boiler room [engine] of this church." One interesting account catches the obvious grip of prayer in Spurgeon's life. In 1887, he was visited by the American theologian Augustus Strong and the Christian businessman John D. Rockefeller. Following the visit, both men agreed the secret of Spurgeon's ministry was that "above all else, he seemed to be a man of prayer."[5]

Like Barnabas, Spurgeon believed prayer was indispensable to walking with and serving God. "Prayer moves the arm that moves the world," Spurgeon was known to say.[6] All the other people mentioned in Acts 13:1—Simeon (called Niger), Lucius (of Cyrene), Manaen (a childhood friend of Herod the tetrarch), and Saul (aka Paul)—sat under a leader who prioritized prayer. Barnabas modeled influence from a posture of prayer.

Godly influencers develop by example. They are hands-on!

THE BARNABAS WAY THROUGH YOU

Acts records the spread of the gospel geographically, socially, and sacrificially. In this first missionary journey, the offer of salvation moved across vast tracts of land at the ends-of-the-earth portion of the book (geographically). We also see the gospel move to all sorts of people (socially): Jews and Gentiles, men and women, rich and poor, ill and healthy. The offer of salvation excludes no one. And we also see that the gospel spread with hardship (sacrificially). Barnabas and Paul endured hardship and covered around 1,500 miles in an era when you couldn't catch a plane or a taxi. It was mainly travel on foot—wearing sandals!

In this portion of the Scriptures, we see that Barnabas possessed several important skills all godly influencers need to nurture to represent God in the world today. One of these was cross-cultural intelligence. He was able to work in multiple settings and among different people groups. If you are to take the gospel to the ends of the earth or across the street, you will need cross-cultural intelligence too. You will need to observe how others from different cultures think, what they value, and how to position yourself near them to show the gospel in all its beauty. Of course, representing God in the world we live in today will also include relational intelligence, that ability to work well with others, to get along and even to coach those around us as we reach out to those beyond them. And this we all must do. As Jesus declared, "The harvest is plentiful, but the workers are few" (Luke 10:2). The twenty-first century still needs harvest workers like Carey, Wishart, Knox, and Barnabas. The twenty-first century needs you.

If we are to plod and mentor as we obey God's call, we would benefit from applying William Carey's most famous two-point sermon to our lives; it's from Isaiah 54:2–3.[7] It's known as the "Deathless Sermon" because Carey preached it to motivate God's people to reach the world for God. It's simply this:

1. Expect great things of God.
2. Attempt great things for God.

Barnabas expected God to reach the world, so he attempted great things for God. We must as well—together.

Some Food for Thought

ONCE AGAIN, REMEMBER TO INVEST SOME TIME reviewing and reflecting on the main ideas in this chapter before attempting to answer the following questions:

1. Making disciples is not easy. Historically, hardship opposes attempts to represent Christ (remember Carey, Wishart, Knox). How would you rate your commitment to making followers of Jesus? Do you persevere when difficulty flares up?

2. Barnabas stepped up to lead, stepped aside to mentor, and stepped back to follow. What does this model to you as you serve God?

3. Serving God requires cross-cultural and relational intelligence. We must be able to work beyond what is familiar and comfortable to us and with different types of people. How would you develop this type of lifestyle and skill?

CHAPTER 6

Guardians and Catalysts

Standing for Truth and Directing Change

The truth will set you free.
JESUS

*My conscience is held captive to the Word
of God. Here I stand. God help me.*
MARTIN LUTHER

REVOCO! RECANT! WILL YOU TAKE BACK WHAT YOU wrote?"

All heads turned to observe the response. It was like a verbal tennis ball slammed over the net at an opponent. They held their breath with eyes fixed on the rebel German monk. Surely, he would renounce what he had written!

The eyes of the average German Joe had looked to him in hope for many years. To them, this monk was no rebel; he was a messiah-like figure hell-bent on liberating them from the pope in Rome. But the eyes on him in this large room were those of foes, not friends. They were the eyes of European princes, dukes, bishops, and archbishops dressed in all their glorious pomp. They were upset that someone was rocking their comfortable boat. Even the king of the Western world looked on. They awaited the signal. Answer the question: *"Revoco?* Recant?" Just say "No!" Then they could all go out for a big bonfire and watch the pesky German monk burn.

And there he stood: Martin Luther. It's April 1521, Worms, Germany. Luther stood before the powers that be, including Emperor Charles V seated on a makeshift throne. Here was the monk who mocked the pope. Would he also defy the king to his face? Ever since Luther's Ninety-Five Theses had fired cannonballs across the Alps at Rome in 1517, pretty much everything else he wrote went viral too. Forty of his works lie on the table before this court. That's what Luther was being asked to revoke. All he had to admit was that it was all a big (bad) joke.

Luther acknowledged the works on the table were his. But then the cheeky rascal informed them there were also many, many more. Now, that's a gutsy bloke! But this courage was not new. For years Luther poked fun at the pope. This monk kept using the Bible to step on the pope's holy toes. It started by exposing the "buy your ticket to heaven" scam used to build the pope's homes. It included public debates with the pope's delegates. Luther even ridiculed one of the pope's theologians, saying he knew God's Word "like a donkey knows to play the lyre"[1] (except Luther used an alternative choice word for a donkey to drive the point home).

Luther stood before them all in his woolly robe. Things didn't look too good. He knew the likely outcome; he was toast! After all, before arrival at this gathering, his friend Spalatin told him that awaiting him in Worms "there were as many Devils as tiles on a roof."[2] And then there was the well-known nickname for him that was a clue as to how things were going to unfold. They called him "the great master of heretics."[3] Luther knew it never ended well for alleged heretics in meetings like these. He knew about John Huss (d. 1415), Jerome of Prague (d. 1416), and Savonarola (d. 1498). This is where they had once stood. All of them, like Luther, were seminary preaching profs (now that makes *me* nervous), and a bonfire always followed next. Preachers seem to burn well.

Interestingly—and whether it's true or not we'll never know—John Huss (the name Huss in his native Bohemian means "goose") made a playful prediction as he sang while he burned a century before. He told his executioner, "Today you burn a goose [a *huss*], but in a hundred years God will raise up a man whose calls for reform cannot be suppressed." Luther's words had gone viral 102 years on!

So, let's get back to Worms that day in April 1521.

"*Revoco!* Recant! Will you take back what you wrote?"

Luther finally spoke. His knees didn't knock. His voice didn't shake. It's as though this guy lived what he wrote in the hymn—a mighty fortress is our God! The truth Luther stood for that day split Western history into the Roman Catholic and Protestant Churches. He said,

> I am bound to the Scriptures I have quoted and my conscience is held captive to the Word of God. I cannot and will not retract anything since it is neither safe nor right to go against conscience. I cannot do otherwise. Here I stand. God help me.[4]

Just to be clear, that's a big, fat, emphatic no!

TRUTH ABOVE ALL

Truth is under attack today too. It isn't surprising, really. The assault on truth is as ancient as the Serpent's words to Eve, our first mom: "Did God really say . . . ?" Satan's age-old tactic is to challenge the words of God.

The aggression of this evil attack has taken a new approach in recent times. The *Oxford English Dictionary*'s choice for Word of the Year in 2016 says it all. It was *post-truth*. Post-truth is where "objective facts are less influential in shaping public opinion than appeals to emotion and personal belief."[5] Basically, truth is whatever you feel, not the actual facts. If I feel it is true, then it is. If I don't feel it, it isn't true. Increasingly, the spirit of the age is to view truth not as facts that are before me but what I want to construct that suits me—whatever I want it to be. And you can do the same. There really is no such thing as truth in this scenario, because you can build your own truth and I can make mine. It's all relative. What we end up with are 7.8 billion personal truths. There is no absolute truth. Hence, we are past that; we are *post*-truth.

Post-truth would be laughable if it were not so rampant and dangerous. Just think about what this is doing to education, morality, law and order, the economy, interpersonal relationships between genders and races, and so on. And what is perhaps the cause of the biggest smile on Satan's face these days as he runs rampant with this new attack on knowing what God says? It is the effect this outlook is having on the Christian church—on everyday believers. In Western societies, there is a mass exodus from Christian truth.[6] And many who remain in the pews are quite slippery on the teachings of the historic Christian faith.

I've been a part of Christian communities in several

countries over the last four decades. I grew up as a pastor's kid in Spain to missionary parents from Northern Ireland. I attended boarding school in Belfast, Northern Ireland, for many years and was part of a church there. I then went on to college in Edinburgh, Scotland, followed by seminary in Texas. The Lord then took me back to Northern Ireland to pastor a church before returning me once again all the way back to Texas to pastor and teach. It's been quite the journey. One of the upsides of it all has been the exposure to God's people in many different places. It is beautiful to show up in a foreign country, enter a Christian church, and have immediate family! But there's been a clear downside. All those years of engagement in all those Christian communities allows me to make the following observation: Christians are weakening drastically in their understanding of basic biblical truth despite having more access to the Bible than any other Christian generation before. We're slipping and sliding on the historic teachings of the Christian faith.

But the truth still matters. The Russian novelist and survivor of the brutal gulags, Alexander Solzhenitsyn, borrowed from an old Russian proverb to remind us of this: "One word of truth shall outweigh the whole world."[7] As a new age of change dawns, followers of Jesus Christ today—like our predecessors Huss, Jerome, Savonarola, and Luther—must guard what God actually said. We are to stand firm on truth. Rather than drifting ignorantly and becoming complicit in Satan's post-truth assault, godly influencers are to be channels of truth and its implications for life.

Truth matters. And godly influencers, like that pesky German monk Luther, are both its guardians and the catalysts of necessary reform through it. We, too, are to protect the gospel. We are to bring about the right changes and applications in light of God's truth into this new age.

THE BARNABAS WAY

Like Luther, Barnabas guarded God's truth through the ups and downs of changing times at the dawn of the church age. Whereas Luther was a guardian of truth and a catalyst for reform (correcting the deviations from God's truth in the past), Barnabas served as a guardian and catalyst for renewal (guiding the implications of God's truth into the church age in light of the changes brought about by the death, burial, and resurrection of Jesus Christ). Either way, Barnabas modeled for everyday believers and aspiring servant leaders two more principles to embrace in Acts 15.

Acts 15 records a massive moment in Christian history: the first church council, known as the Jerusalem Council, around AD 50. It is a defining moment in church history because a crucial decision was made that protected the gospel of Jesus Christ. The gathering guarded truth and managed a transition moment very well. And Barnabas was a key player in this momentous event.

Barnabas and Paul returned to the church in Antioch full of joy and great reports following their joint missionary journey (Acts 14:26–28). God was at work. Men and women were believing in Jesus Christ despite much opposition. But eventually disturbing reports came from those churches. It appears others followed on the heels of Barnabas and Paul, adding to the gospel of faith alone in Jesus Christ alone. It is quite likely that Paul wrote his first letter at this point: Galatians. The letter drips with a strong tone and a clear message against adding anything to the work of salvation in Jesus Christ. Paul would not have it. This was a serious issue. The gospel was subtly tweaked, and that was wrong.

The same issue occurred in Antioch:

> Certain people came down from Judea to Antioch and were teaching the believers: "Unless you are circumcised, according to the custom taught by Moses, you cannot be saved." This brought Paul and Barnabas into sharp dispute and debate with them. So Paul and Barnabas were appointed, along with some other believers, to go up to Jerusalem to see the apostles and elders about this question. (Acts 15:1–2)

In Antioch, there was no need for a letter. Paul and Barnabas confronted these fake teachers head-on and in person. The escalation of the situation was such, however, that the issue was sent on up to Jerusalem for a decision from the overall leaders of the church. And so Barnabas and Paul headed to Jerusalem for the first official council of the Christian church.

The scene of Acts 15:1–35 breaks down into three movements:

- Doctrinal problem emerges in Antioch (Acts 15:1–5)
- Debate and decision reached in Jerusalem (Acts 15:6–21)
- Dissemination of decision to all churches (Acts 15:22–35)

Barnabas emerged in each of these sections. In the first, Barnabas, along with Paul, was one of the key players keen to snuff out the false teaching entering the church in Antioch. He was also selected to go and resolve the issue in Jerusalem. In the second section, Barnabas contributed to the debate surrounding the issue alongside church heavyweights like Peter and James. In the final move, Barnabas was one of the official delegates entrusted by the church with broadcasting the decision reached across all churches.

As we zoom in on Barnabas's specific involvement in this historic event, two more principles appear for us to copy today.

The Barnabas Way Guards Truth

Godly influencers are guardians of truth. They are passionate about truth. Like Luther, we all stand in a world like Worms every day. Truth is under assault and not just from outside the church. Just as in Acts 15, attacks can come from inside the church too. It's a subtle assault. A firm, unapologetic, and respectful stance is needed. All followers of Jesus be warned: this *is* costly. It's always been so!

The history of the Christian faith testifies to how costly standing for truth is. Take one example: a twenty-two-year-old rich girl called Perpetua. She was imprisoned in AD 203 in Carthage, a great Mediterranean city on the northern coast of Africa. The reason for her incarceration? She was a Christian. The Roman emperor's birthday was coming up soon, and someone thought it would be fun to publicly sacrifice Christians as part of the birthday celebrations. Perpetua's dad desperately pleaded with her to turn her back on her faith—just for a little

> **BARNABAS PRINCIPLE #10:**
> **TRUTH**
>
> A godly influencer is resolute for the absolute.

while, even to pretend to do so, crossed fingers behind the back and all that. God would understand. Moreover, she had a little baby to rear.

But Perpetua couldn't recant her faith. She handed her little baby over to her dad and pointed at a pot. "See that pot, Dad?" she said. "Can you call it by any other name? No. It's a pot. Well, I am a Christian. I can't be called by any other name; that is who I am." Perpetua, and other believers with her, were cut with knives then let loose in an arena as a spectacle. Then a wild boar, a bear, and a leopard were let loose on them. She died in the arena that day, but she stood firm for the truth.[8]

Truth matters. Truth matters to followers of Jesus Christ set on influencing the world. This is what Barnabas believed and modeled for us.

Barnabas was a doctrinal watchdog. He guarded biblical truth. Barnabas understood the need to constantly keep an eye on what Satan will do to God's words. He twists things. It's always back to that "Did God really say?" approach. As the gospel spread, Barnabas and Paul hit the pause button to straighten out a tweak made to the gospel as it applies to Gentiles (non-Jews). Must a Gentile adopt a Jewish lifestyle before he can become a Christian by faith? This was a big issue then. Barnabas said no. Note three important issues he modeled.

First, Barnabas detected error because he knew truth. You can detect falsehood only if you know truth. This was a subtle falsehood creeping in, which is why it was so dangerous. And it is understandable why it crept in. It seemed to have the history of God's people (Israel) to back it up as well as chapter and verse to appeal to in the Hebrew Bible. They were all trying to figure out what changes come about because of the death, burial, and resurrection of Jesus Christ.

From the perspective of the false teachers, the issue boiled down to this: Yes, salvation is by God's grace through faith in Jesus, *but* those who are really, truly saved live according to the law of Moses—including circumcision. Didn't God give Moses the Law? Didn't God give Israel circumcision? This is the way the righteous have always lived. Non-Jews who become followers of Jesus need to go the full Jewish route to be saved: They need to live like Jews, right?

Wrong! Barnabas detected the error. He knew what was wrong and didn't underestimate its danger. He was wise enough to know that it is always better to overestimate a potential danger than to underestimate it.

In the Battle of Britain during World War II, the Nazi air force attacked Britain. The British Royal Air Force withstood the assault. A reason for this success was overestimation on the part of the British and underestimation on the part of the Nazis. Each interpreted the size of the other's squadron of planes according to their own internal criteria. A squadron for the Nazis had twelve planes. For the British, it had twenty planes. So, the Nazis underestimated how many planes the British were sending up in each squadron. They thought these were squadrons of twelve when in fact they were of twenty. They got overconfident. The British, however, overestimated how many the Nazis had in the air (twenty in each squadron when in fact there were only twelve) and so were overcautious. Ultimately, Barnabas did something similar here. He was not going to underestimate the potential damage of subtle tweaks to the gospel.

Second, Barnabas dealt with error head-on. Barnabas and Paul spoke up. They didn't just pray and hope it would go away. They didn't simply abstain from going to that Sunday school class because of questionable teaching. They knew the danger of that little bit of yeast Jesus warned about (Matthew 16:6). That took courage and conviction. It presumably began with some uncomfortable conversations that then escalated to debate. But like American founding father Thomas Jefferson allegedly said, "As it relates to style, swim with the current. But as it relates to principles, stand solid as a rock." Barnabas was not going to let the church get carried along with that current. It was time to stand firm like a rock.

Lastly, Barnabas deputized through the right channels. Barnabas and Paul were sent as representatives to the leadership in Jerusalem. They were God's appointed leaders. And Barnabas and Paul were also official delegates of the leadership in Jerusalem who broadcasted the decision. An orderly process was followed, as we will see shortly. After all, these were changing times. Order fends off chaos. An orderly process is wise.

All in all, godly influencers stand firm on, and for, the truth; an authentic life of influence for Christ is resolute for the absolute. Absolute truth matters.

The Barnabas Way Directs Good Change

Change is stable. I know that sounds like a contradiction, but it's not. Change is *always* happening. It lurks around every corner. Change is a constant. Benjamin Franklin gets credit for noting that the only thing that is certain in life is death and taxes. But author Martin Orridge is right in noting that "in this world nothing is certain but *change*, death, and taxes."[9]

We have a bit of a love-hate relationship with change. Some change we embrace, such as when we are bored with life or if there is a reward to obtain. But some change is unwelcome, particularly that which threatens our sense of control, like job changes or the loss of a loved one or a global virus. That change produces stress and anxiety. It's why the stress management industry is so profitable. Some change we just flat-out fear because it is unknown.

Take the potato as an example. I'm Northern Irish. I had a whiskey quip earlier. I need a potato one too. Did you know the potato is not native to Ireland or Europe? It appears the Peruvians were having fries long before the French. The potato came from South America into Europe in the sixteenth century. That's quite recent.

....

BARNABAS PRINCIPLE #11:
CHANGE

A godly influencer
manages change well.

....

And here is the remarkable thing: when first introduced by Sir Walter Raleigh, newspapers printed articles demonizing it, the general public rejected it, and pastors preached sermons against it. It was new, strange, and different—probably evil— therefore, it was to be feared. We eventually figured out how to cook it and keep it company with ketchup. Now it's a staple food across the world. Some good changes we resist because of fear.

Godly influencers must handle change well, especially good change. All transition has a level of risk, after all. Barnabas not only modeled how to stop people from changing truth but also was a key player in managing good changes occurring in the church because of God's revealed truth.

Barnabas was part of a process that managed change well. We would do well to adapt and customize the process Barnabas followed. Processes are important. It's valuable to have a plan, formal or informal. This first church council presented some godly guidelines for managing good changes well. At some point, read Acts 15 with these guidelines in mind.

First, the issue was dealt with immediately and appropriately (Acts 15:1–5). Paul and Barnabas gauged the danger of the issue. As we saw earlier, this was a period of transition in God's unfolding plan. And this was an issue concerning the implications of the gospel. Immediate action was necessary. And so they headed up through the right channels to the right people—the leaders of the church in Jerusalem—to manage the tension created by these changing times.

Second, the issue was discussed patiently and courteously (Acts 15:6–12). Several voices spoke into the situation. Everyone got a turn. They teased out the issue through their experiences, understanding it theologically, socially, and ethnically. All angles were looked at and thought through. Feelings and experiences were welcome but they were led by facts, all with a respectful tone.

Third, the issue was determined decisively and scripturally (Acts 15:13–21). James put words to the council's clear conclusion. The Scriptures guided the verdict. The quest was to understand whether the changes before them, including the experiences described, were in keeping with God's Word. They were! What the Bible said was central.

Fourth, the verdict was disseminated officially and practically (Acts 15:22–35). The council's decision was communicated to all the churches by official and reliable representatives, including Barnabas. It was not left to word of mouth; they used the only medium of mass communication they had at the time: paper. No emails. No Facebook. No Twitter. The letter carried by hand from church to church even included practical advice for avoiding tensions on secondary matters that could corrupt.

And finally, as a bonus, the verdict also warned of the existence of dissidents (Acts 15:24). Basically, expect difficult people out there. There are always a few in the church. They never go away!

There will be changes in your church, your relationships, your workplace. These will test you as others watch on. Godly influencers today learn to manage change well.

THE BARNABAS WAY THROUGH YOU

Barnabas was a guardian of truth and a catalyst for good changes occurring in the church. God's everyday Christians charged with influencing the world would serve Christ well by copying his way.

We are to be people of the Word. False teaching is still creeping in through believers who are not rooted in the Word. A recent study by Lifeway Research indicates that most Americans who love the Bible don't read it.[10] That's startling. And it is revealing. It's no surprise that issues rejected through-out Christian history are now increasingly ushered to the front pew in church these days. It is a blend of ignorance of truth and this whole post-truth movement we are drifting toward. In a world where fake news, misinformation, and artificial intelligence are on the rise, Barnabas calls for a certain type of aptitude: truth intelligence. As Jesus declared, only the truth sets you free (John 8:32). Don't forget that life unraveled into slavery to sin because of a lie: "Did God really say . . . ?" Truth matters!

It is also essential you and I see the types of changes on the horizon so that we can respond to these well. Change is constant. There is no need to panic or run. Some of it we must reject. But other changes we direct or even bring about as catalysts or as reformers like Luther. These changes we manage well. And Barnabas shows us how.

In short, you can be a catalyst of good and necessary change that protects God's truth along the way. You can help this generation understand the implications of the true gospel in these changing times. I don't know if you've ever thought of this as your responsibility as a follower of Jesus, but it is. It's not just the role of your pastor to know truth to the extent of being able to defend it and detect subtle distortions of it. You, too, must stand for truth well. God may not call you to die for Him as Perpetua did, but He wants you to live for Him. And living for Jesus today when everyone operates on a "my truth" default setting means men and women who, like Luther, stand for truth with boldness and direct good change in living out that stance.

Some Food for Thought

AFTER THINKING YOUR WAY THROUGH THE MAIN teachings in this chapter, answer the following questions:

1. Have you ever studied the culture in which you live? The tentacles of a postmodern and post-truth assault are everywhere. It's time to put your finger on the pulse of cultural trajectories to stand firm on God's truth. How can you study culture?

2. Truth assaults occur inside the church, not just outside our doors. Acts 15 emerges from an in-house attack on the gospel. What does it take to detect such subtle encroachments? What would developing truth intelligence involve?

3. Ministry leaders encounter change regularly. It is important to learn to manage change well. What do you think is essential to manage change well?

CHAPTER 7

Troubleshooters and Recyclers

Defusing Tension and Redeeming Failure

*Come to me, all you who are
weary and burdened.*
JESUS

*Leaders don't inflict pain;
they bear pain.*
MAX DE PREE

IT WAS DEEP INTO THE NIGHT. MY BROTHERS, DAD, and I were sitting around the kitchen table having a great laugh. We were telling good old stories from decades past. What a wonderful evening around the fire, one I'd love to relive! Our trip down memory lane took us to so-and-so who did such and such years ago. Most stories came from life around the Spanish villages where Mom and Dad pastored. We'd grown up there as kids but our recollections were fragmented. We brought up old memories, and Dad filled in the details with a running commentary along the way. These fill-ins were often funny.

Dad explained why, for example, fugitives would show up at our door at night. Father Murphy (as they called him) visited them as prisoners weekly, so if they ever escaped they would knock on the door of their only friend for help. He also filled us in on why he was regularly seen doing dodgy business deals with local drug addicts at the corner of the town square. He was buying back *our own items* from those rascals who'd broken into our home the night before and robbed us as we slept! Now his boys were adults—all in ministry—so we could handle Dad connecting all those old dots. The stories were brilliant; most were rib-tickling. We laughed and laughed and laughed long into the night.

But things took a turn: "Dad, are you OK?" I leaned across

the kitchen table toward him. I was nervous. Was Dad having a heart attack?

Dad finally drew a deep breath. He held his hands at his chest, then slowly gave us the thumbs-up. He was OK. Phew! He was laughing so hard that tears were gushing down his face and he was struggling to catch a breath. For a split second, we were worried all the laughing was escorting Dad to an early grave.

The conversation then turned to a lady in our church back then; let's call her Gi. She had been my Sunday school teacher since I was a little boy. She was a key church member who'd been discipled—like a daughter—by Mom and Dad for many years. Gi was like a big sister to us in many ways. Our recollections from long ago raised some funny and intriguing details needing to be filled in.

We remembered that every Sunday evening Gi would make her way to the front of the church during the service. Her husband followed in hot pursuit, armed with a guitar. She'd be dressed like a flamenco dancer. He'd play like a Spanish guitar maestro. Gi looked like an angel but, if truth be told, when she sang, the neighborhood dogs howled. Trust me, I'm being kind. Then she'd take her seat a few rows from the front only to rise and leave as Dad's sermon began. Gi was always back and seated just in time for the final hymn and for all the fun in the church hall that followed the evening service. We laughed as we recalled detail after detail of this intriguing weekly act. It was Gi's own religious ritual.

But then one day, the Sunday evening dog-howling stopped. Gi was gone. We never saw her again. Dad?

We turned to Dad for his next out-of-this-world funny fill-in. Tears were flowing down his face again, but this time he gripped his head in his hands. We quickly realized these tears sprung from a different well, one deep down in his heart. Those tears told a different story, one that was still out of this world but *not* funny. This was decades-old pain bubbling through.

After a few moments, Dad spoke. He spoke of Gi's coming to faith. He spoke of years raising her in the faith, marrying her to the guitar expert, and serving alongside her in evangelism in our town. For years she was a lay leader. Gi taught Sunday school, she sang (well, sort of!), led youth camps, and represented the church in community outreach events. And then one day a woman from the village came looking for her. This woman was raging mad, repeatedly asking, "Where is that whore? Where is your harlot?" You can imagine the confusion for Mom and Dad. The lady proceeded to explain how the village knew Gi as the local wayward woman. She ranted and raved about how deplorable it was that the church endorsed sexual acts as part of worship services. Mom and Dad were just stunned. Decades of ministry in this area, and this is what the people thought? Why would she say that?

As it turns out, the furious woman was right. This is why my dad still hurt so deeply. Every Sunday evening service following her grand, dog-howling solo and just as the sermon began, Gi left the church service to meet her lovers (yes, plural). *That* was her weekly irreligious ritual. And a few in the town knew this well. Who were some of her lovers? Two men of the church who excused themselves from the service in turns. Their plan worked for years, the guilty parties knowing their spouses sat unaware in the church service listening to the Word of God. That's where Dad's hurt sprung from. Many years later, it was still sore.

Investing yourself in people is messy and dangerous. People lash out. People grab and fight and grumble and stray. People can disappoint. Pastors know this all too well. So do parents. While there are lots of good moments along the way, influencing others up close brings pain. Leaders hurt because leadership harms. Influencing people is messy and dangerous stuff.

NEVER TRUST A LEADER WITHOUT A LIMP

Investing in those around you comes with bumps and bruises along the way. Kids, work colleagues, neighbors, other Christians—it's all the same. There are tough decisions, tricky problems, unfair criticism, unending stresses and strains. Of course, there is also lots of fun and joy, but then we rush back to all those aches and pains. Influencing another life takes its toll. Someone always feels wronged by whatever decision you make. It is easy to get frustrated or disillusioned, feel lonely, or become insecure. In *Leading with a Limp*, Dan Allender says it well: "Leading is very likely the most costly thing you will ever do."[1]

Although influencing others can hurt, pain can teach. Painful experiences are perhaps the greatest professors.

Certainly, this is the case in any form of influence over people, including leadership of an organization. All those wounds and scars can be put to good use. Wisdom often flourishes in the soil of hurt. Samuel Chand's book is worth checking out based on the title alone: *Leadership Pain: The Classroom for Growth.* His title makes my entire point. Here is wisdom in one line: "Leadership is both brutal and beautiful. It's *bleedership*! It's *brutiful*!"[2] As wonderful as it is to influence another life for God, be warned: it is a magnet for pain.[3]

And it is precisely because of these aches and pains that godly influencers, whether everyday pastors or parents, can help others navigate life with God. The greatest leaders do tend to walk with a stick. J. Robert Clinton's advice is wise: never trust a leader who doesn't walk with a limp.[4]

THE BARNABAS WAY

Barnabas understood the difficult sides of influencing others for Christ. He walked with a limp. Like the great ancient theologian, Basil of Caesarea, Barnabas could be said to have an ambidextrous faith.[5] He held life's hurts and difficulties in one hand and God's blessings and purposes in the other. He believed God worked through both: through thick and thin. In Acts 15:36–41, Barnabas acted as a problem solver and a people launcher. It's exciting to influence another life, but you've got to be able to troubleshoot their problems and recycle their failures in order to launch them God's way.

In a previous chapter, when dealing with people's potential, I quoted Max De Pree, who wrote, "Three of the key elements in the art of working together are how to deal with change, how to deal with conflict, and how to reach our potential."[6] In the following verses, we see this wise observation enacted. Barnabas modeled for us how to adapt in light of relational tensions and conflict in order to maximize someone's ministry or life potential. We must learn to do this well because tension and conflict are guaranteed. Let's examine these verses:

> Some time later Paul said to Barnabas, "Let us go back and visit the believers in all the towns where we preached the word of the Lord and see how they are doing." Barnabas wanted to take John, also called Mark, with them, but Paul did not think it wise to take him, because he had deserted them in Pamphylia and had not continued with them in the work. They had such a sharp disagreement that they parted company. Barnabas took Mark and sailed for Cyprus, but Paul chose Silas and left, commended by the believers to the grace of the Lord. He went through Syria and Cilicia, strengthening the churches. (Acts 15:36–41)

A few days after protecting the gospel at the Jerusalem Council, Paul's plan was to take another missionary journey with Barnabas. His desire was for this to be a pastoral trip rather than an expedition to proclaim the gospel. He wanted to visit those recent believers we read about in Acts 13–14.

A problem arose between Barnabas and Paul concerning

what to do with John Mark. It was a practical problem—a staffing issue. This tension was relational, not doctrinal, missional, or moral. Barnabas wanted to bring another apprentice with them, John Mark, but Paul did not. The reason for Paul's objection is understandable. John Mark was with them on the first journey, but he left them early on during this trip, which didn't sit well with Paul (Acts 13:13). We don't know why he left them, and suggestions are all over the place, including that John Mark missed Mom's home cooking (which is an understandable reason if his mom cooked like mine!). What we do know is that John Mark abandoned Paul and Barnabas when they needed him. Paul was right. John Mark had a failed track record.

The strain on the relationship between Paul and Barnabas in Acts 15 does show us a pathway forward beyond the problem. The tension was resolved. While Barnabas and Paul differed sharply on the matter, it was only a disagreement about what to do with John Mark. This wasn't a big bust-up between godly men that left both storming off in a huff. This was a clear-cut difference of opinion on a practical ministry matter by godly men focusing on personal preferences that may even be revealing of their own personalities: a people-focused Barnabas at odds with a task-focused Paul.

Many years ago, I sat with Dr. Howard "Prof" Hendricks in his office at Dallas Theological Seminary. We were talking about our mutual biblical hero, Barnabas. Prof knew I was a fan of Barnabas and was researching his life a little in my master's program. I still remember as clear as crystal his final words in our conversation. They were his thoughts on this very scene in Scripture. I believe they also spoke of Prof's lifelong ministry emphasis. He said, "Jonathan, Paul chose the work. Barnabas chose the worker."

Prof Hendricks was right. God used this incident to accomplish His purposes: two missionary expeditions emerge according to two styles of ministry. And interestingly, both headed for home to begin ministry there. Barnabas sailed home to Cyprus with John Mark. Paul took Silas and went to Cilicia, which is where his home of Tarsus was. The offshoot of both paths is remarkable, as we will see in the next chapter. At this point, though, what we see is that God used the split; He redeemed the tension to direct His servants to new ministry fields.

This is the last scene in Acts featuring Barnabas, but it presents us with two relevant principles of godly influence for everyday Christians to copy.

The Barnabas Way Deals with Conflict

Conflict comes for all sorts of reasons: personality clashes, misunderstanding, differences of opinion, ego. The list is endless. The history of humankind is a story of one crisis after another, and the responses tend to be as varied as the causes: avoid it, fight it, give in to it, put up with it, resolve it. It takes wisdom to know how to deal with each situation in a fitting way. If often seems there is no win-win at all, especially if you are in a leadership role like a pastor with quarreling parishioners or a parent with squabbling kids. Someone always ends up declaring, "That's not fair!"

Take poor King Oswiu as an example. The year is AD 664. It's another cold, wet, and windswept day in what is modern-day northern England. The occasion is an ancient conference, the Synod of Whitby. Oswiu, the king of Northumbria, sits listening to the back-and-forth bickering of two age-old rival groups. After the constant squabbling he must rule in favor of one, knowing the other will take offense; it really is another lose-lose for him.

. . . .

BARNABAS PRINCIPLE #12:
CONFLICT

A godly influencer
handles tension well.

. . . .

Who are these rivals before him? Monks! Worse actually, Irish monks versus English monks. Good luck, Oswiu! Two issues dominate this pastors' conference. The first is conflict over the correct date to celebrate Easter. That's right. More monks with "dating" issues. The English group represents a branch of Roman Christianity and wants to follow the pope. After all, Saint Peter is the boss of the church on earth, right? You don't mess with the one who holds the keys to the kingdom of God. The Irish, on the other hand, want to follow Celtic Christian traditions given their personal spiritual father is Saint Columba. Charges of heresy and excommunication fly across the room. Yet the difference in these Easter calculations is just a few days.

Now to the second issue for King Oswiu on that prickly synod agenda. Is it the Trinity? Salvation in Christ? The authority of the Scriptures? No. No. And, no. As if the first issue wasn't a headache enough, the second is also painful for Oswiu. It is cast as an issue of holy service to God: basically, how dedicated are you to Him? That's an important issue. But the discussion concerns dedication via tonsures. What on earth are tonsures? Well, simply put, tonsures are hairstyles! No joke. This king has to rule on holy haircuts. He is to provide the answer to the all-important question, What hairstyle does God prefer? Don't dismiss this as silly nonsense that Oswiu himself should dismiss. The issue is splitting Christianity in his domain. Should a monk shave a circle (a bald spot on top) at the crown of the head like Roman Christianity? Or is it better to shave the front from ear over to ear (like a receding hairline) just as the Celtic monks prefer? Poor King Oswiu! It is lose-lose again.

Ultimately, King Oswiu must decide. That's what leaders do. He rules in favor of the English-Roman pastors, making enemies of the Irish lot. That's a dangerous move. But why did Oswiu rule as he did? Well, because Saint Peter's relics (basically, his bones in Rome) are holier than Saint Columba's in Iona.[7] Smart guy! Of course, there's the practical wisdom of not messing with the guy you believe has the keys that open and close *your* door to the kingdom of heaven. Poor Oswiu didn't stand a chance of coming out of this conference a happy guy. Leaders hurt because they deal with people, and people are a dangerous lot.

Godly influencers must learn to handle conflict well; it *is* coming. They must deal with it in a godly manner, particularly relational tensions that develop with those around you, be it at home, at work, or at church. Conflicts in these relationships are worth resolving. In our scene, Barnabas and Paul encountered a ministerial obstacle. How they handled it passes on good, practical advice for us to adopt.

When conflict emerged, Barnabas and Paul clarified the problem. They didn't panic; they started problem-solving. Identifying the problem is the first and necessary step toward a godly resolution. It is asking and answering the question, What are we dealing with here? What is the real problem? Let's talk things out. Both men had the same goal: another godly expedition. The pursuit was godly, so it was not a disagreement over vision. It also was not a doctrinal conflict. They stood together on truth. Nor was it a moral problem. This conflict centered on a practical side of ministry—a how-to aspect of ministry. In this case, it was diagnosed specifically as a relational obstacle—that staffing issue with John Mark.

When conflict emerged, Barnabas and Paul voiced their desired outcomes. Both men expressed how they believed the issue should move forward. They didn't escalate the situation by storming off in a huff. The backstory of the disagreement (John Mark's track record) was evident to both. How to deal with that moving into a similar ministry situation was the disagreement. Because of their relationship, each man expressed their view on what was to be done. Barnabas wanted to take John Mark. Paul didn't. Each knew where the other stood.

When conflict emerged, Barnabas and Paul agreed on a way forward. Both men saw a way forward within each of their respective callings inside the big picture of the Great Commission. For Barnabas, the big picture was *future* focused: developing an individual person for long-term ministry leadership. For Paul, it was *present* focused: spreading the gospel to all persons now in this next expedition. In this case, they agreed to disagree. The sharp disagreement was over the practical issue. That's it. Nothing more. A way forward was settled. On this ministry issue, each would go with their desired path forward. They stepped away with clear and different plans. And that was OK!

When conflict emerged, Barnabas and Paul remained on the same side. While they physically parted company, they continued to pursue the same overall vision: a missionary expedition. Each one knew that the other's role was not his own personal role. There was no burning of relational bridges. They parted peacefully. This was a practical problem, after all. There is plenty of room for divergences of opinion on *how* to carry out the Great Commission. In this case, the resolution did not mean going in one direction or the other, but both. It meant they parted ways with mutual respect for each other's choices, albeit from a distance.

In St. Patrick's Cathedral, Dublin, there is a remarkable door on display. It preaches a practical message on conflict resolution dating all the way back to AD 1492. Back then, two important families in Dublin were at loggerheads over who held the top-ranking public office: Lord Deputy. The disagreement turned violent, and one of the families, the Butlers, took refuge in the Chapter House of Saint Patrick's Cathedral.

The FitzGerald family followed them in hot pursuit. They claimed to want peace. But it was a big risk for the Butlers to believe this was true and simply open the door. What if these words of peace were just that, words? The FitzGeralds ordered a hole be cut open on the wooden door. Then, one of them put his arm through the hole to offer a handshake as an act of good faith to the Butlers on the other side. The Butlers, seeing the willingness to risk an arm, grabbed hold of the hand and shook it in peace. And so, this door—still on display as a visual sermon in Dublin—is known as the Door of Reconciliation. From this story emerged the famous Irish expression "to chance his arm."

Conflict is coming. But God can use these strains to direct and redirect His purposes. Moments of painful crises can force good shifts to occur. It depends on how those involved respond. In the situation Barnabas and Paul faced, two missionary expeditions emerged. Both were in keeping with the will of God.

Godly influencers can handle tension well; they *must* handle tension well. The world we seek to shape for Christ is watching.

The Barnabas Way Redeems Mistakes

In 1501, the authorities of the city of Florence stared at a huge marble rock before them in the churchyard. It had been there for decades as a horrible eyesore. What they saw was just a huge, useless stone on which pigeons perched. Some chippings at its base by a previous sculptor seemed proof enough that nothing could be done with this rock. Someone had tried! As a potential statue, this rock was done, ruined, and it couldn't be redone. It just took up space in the yard.

When young Michelangelo looked at that same rock, he saw much more. It was a bit battered but was still a good-looking rock. Michelangelo saw potential waiting to be released. For several years, he "discipled" the lump of rock personally, up close, one-on-one. Every day, with hammer and chisel in hand, he chipped away the rough edges to reveal the potential that lay within. He knew what this discarded piece of rock could become. And then the day of the big reveal came. It was 1504. Those same city leaders who rejected this marble before now gathered for the uncovering of Michelangelo's project. The sheets were removed from the large stone. Standing seventeen feet tall and weighing six tons, none other than King David himself emerged from the veil— perfect, imposing, and finally released from his rocky tomb.

It gets better. Michelangelo captured David as no one had done so before. Here was a young shepherd boy, sling and stone in hand, heading out to slay the giant Goliath and establish himself in history forevermore. All other sculpture depictions of David were of him *after* the moment that propelled him to

....

BARNABAS PRINCIPLE #13:
OPPORTUNITY

A godly influencer never wastes a mistake; instead, they recycle failures.

....

global fame. Michelangelo caught David just *before* the Goliath battle—as a next-to-nobody shepherd boy on the way into the history books. The impact was immediately obvious. This most famous of all statues was not to be placed in the background for pigeons to call it home; it was placed in the front square of Florence. And for nearly five hundred years it stood there until it needed to be sheltered to avoid the bombs of war.[8]

Like Michelangelo with this huge marble rock, Barnabas saw potential in John Mark. All that was needed was a season with a hammer and chisel to chip away a little here and a little there. John Mark had ministry potential. And like a seasoned sports scout with an eye on a young athlete, Barnabas saw an opportunity to launch another talent for God. For him, John Mark was worth the split with Paul. Why?

Barnabas knew God doesn't waste wounds. God recycles our failures. Failures can either paralyze us or be our professors. John Mark made a mistake in the previous missionary expedition. He came to this one with a wounded past, and all those involved knew that well. The question was what to do with him now. As Paul sighed when John Mark put up his hand volunteering for the next ministry venture, Barnabas smiled. Barnabas knew past mistakes could be a tool (like Michelangelo's chisel) to chip away at that which blocked future potential. For John Mark, failure could be a great teacher. It was the road to becoming a great man.

Thomas Edison, America's greatest inventor (the light bulb, electrical distribution, ability to replay music) was a man with a Barnabas-like perspective. He was often asked about the many thousands of failures he had when trying to invent the light bulb. His answer was always the same: "I have not failed. I've just found 10,000 ways that won't work." That's the attitude, Thomas! He saw failures and mistakes as steps forward, not back. Like all of us, Barnabas also made mistakes. We read of one in Galatians 2. But Barnabas knew personally that you can learn from mistakes. Past failures can be put to good use by God.

Barnabas recycled John Mark's failure to relaunch his ministry life. God is willing not only to redeem and restore us despite our failed past but to reuse those who learn from those mistakes. Godly influencers recycle failures in order to relaunch lives in godly directions. There is an optimism about what God can do in a life that is willing and available. It is an opportunity. And Barnabas knew this.

We've seen this already. In past chapters, we saw Barnabas function precisely as he does here. He's the same, consistent role model. He saw potential when others just saw a problematic person. He saw past Paul's failed past. He not only detected potential in Paul despite his dodgy résumé but took a risk on him to personally launch his protégé into ministry work. What we see here is Barnabas being true to form, except now with a new protégé. And he did it without rubbing it in Paul's face. I'd be tempted to say, "Paul, give John Mark a break! You above all people should know. Remember, I saw beyond your risky past. I saw preacher Paul when everyone just saw persecutor Saul. You were an assassin before you were an apostle!"

In a day when we aim to recycle everything, we'd do well not to dispose of people. Rather, we must recycle their failures for God's use. That's what Barnabas shows us here: godly influencers never waste a mistake. They recycle those failures in the people around them.

THE BARNABAS WAY THROUGH YOU

Godly influencers know the pain life brings. But they don't inflict pain on others; rather, they bear pain.[9] Hurt people don't have to hurt people. They don't need to succumb to more difficulties and tension by following a path of hurt, discouragement, and bitterness. Instead, they choose to take it to God. After all, Jesus did say, "Come to me, all you who are weary and burdened, and I will give you rest" (Matthew 11:28).

In doing so, authentic Christians like you can become an oasis that refreshes others who hurt. Because godly influencers have developed a sort of crisis intelligence, they are composed under pressure and are able to troubleshoot problems well. They live and learn from life. They find ways to recycle people's failures and put them to good use. Troubleshooters and recyclers come alongside others. They know that the culture can change one person at a time when godly influencers like this do just that.

Barnabas, like my dad, walked with a limp. As a result, he learned how to fix problems and launch people with questionable and scarred pasts. That's what it takes to release others. That's what it will take for you to launch others to pursue their God-given destinies.

Some Food for Thought

REMEMBER TO SET SOME TIME ASIDE FOR REFLEC-tion on the main teachings in this chapter before answering the following questions:

1. Pouring your life into other people opens you up to hurt. Take some time to face those wounds. List them. Name them. What did you learn from them?
2. Read and reflect on Jesus' teaching in Matthew 11:28–30. He invites you to take your past hurts to Him. Why don't you take them to Him now?
3. Godly servant leaders will deal with many crises. Crisis intelligence is essential. Revisit what you learned in this chapter on how Barnabas handled tension in a God-honoring way.

CHAPTER 8

Farsighted and Followers

A Lasting Legacy, God's Way

Not so with you!
JESUS

You might even have made a name for yourself.
LORD RANDOLPH CHURCHILL

WINSTON S. CHURCHILL WAS STILL FEELING RATHER low. Two years had passed, but the sting of rejection remained. How could he have been ousted from public office as prime minister in 1945 while the nation celebrated his victory over Adolf Hitler in that brutal war? That sort of national rejection cuts deep. In 1947, now in his seventies, he heads down to his little art studio at his country home of Chartwell to try and move on. How does a global leader nurse his wounds? This one paints.

Winston is fixing a portrait of his father, Lord Randolph Churchill, who died decades earlier in 1895 when Winston was only twenty. Randolph had been a national leader himself. He rose to become Leader of the House of Commons and even Chancellor of the Exchequer. These were two positions close to the top of British politics. But Randolph was a tough dad to please, and Winston knew he never measured up. Randolph was too impressed with himself to see any potential in his disappointing son. All that to say, Winston knew rejection well from very early on in life. He just never lived up to anything in the eyes of his dad at home. But here he is in 1947—an old man—busy at work making sure his dad's moustache looks good on canvas as he deals with more hurt.

Enough of my words. Winston's say it best. His essay "The

Dream" was never intended for public view. Only many years later, after Winston's own death, was it published for us all to read. "The Dream" is a fictitious conversation between the veteran global leader, Winston, and the ghost of his long-dead dad in that small art studio in 1947.

Winston wrote, "I was just trying to give the twirl to his moustache when I suddenly felt an odd sensation. I turned around with my palette in my hand, and there, sitting in my red leather upright armchair, was my father. He looked just as I had seen him in his prime."[1]

As the essay unfolds, a fascinating father-son conversation transpires. Winston updates his dad on fifty years of world history—all that happened since Randolph died. He covers the state of the British Empire, two brutal world wars, the rise of socialism, national and international politics, the monarchy, the new American word *OK*, and even an update on my home region of Ulster (Northern Ireland). Randolph remains true to form. He remains condescending of his "disappointing son," although he's quite impressed by all that Winston knows. Winston seems quite informed.

As I read through "The Dream," excitement bubbles up. I can't wait to get to that "gotcha" moment when Winston tells his dad all that he did become. Tell him, Winston. Go on, rub it in his face—bestselling author, decorated soldier, prime minister, greatest Briton! But that moment never comes. Winston tells his dad everything; he recounts everything *except* his own incredible role in it all. Randolph departs as quickly as his ghost appeared, believing his son was just an average man—a next-to-nobody restoration painter—living in an average home.

Randolph's departing words to Winston irritate me a little: "As I listened to you unfolding these fearful facts," he says, "you seemed to know a great deal about them. I never expected that you would develop so far and so fully. Of course, you are too old now to think about such things, but when I hear you talk I really wonder that you didn't go into politics. You might have done a lot to help. You might even have made a name for yourself."[2] And then, just like that, Randolph was gone.

"You might even have made a name for yourself." Are you kidding me, Randolph? You have no idea who your son became! And are you kidding me, Winston? Here was your opportunity (even fictionally) to put those daddy issues behind you. I want to grab Winston's pen and rewrite the end of "The Dream" precisely as history unfolded. Winston wasn't just an average painter living out an average life in an average home; he was the greatest statesman in British history. He is perhaps the reason Randolph's own country survived World War II and still speaks English.

But Winston remains silent. He says nothing! He is clearly having a little fictional fun. We'll never know why Winston doesn't disclose his role in history. Perhaps he no longer actually cares what Dad thinks. Perhaps Dad is just a version of the entire nation that ousted him in 1945—both completely unaware of the legacy Winston left in his wake.

We will never know, and so my irritation—*righteous* irritation—remains. Of the many twists and turns in "The

Dream," the issue of legacy emerges strong. What is a good legacy? What do we want to leave behind? And more importantly, does it really matter whether those around us ever know what great things we've done?

THE QUEST FOR A LASTING LEGACY

Making a name for oneself—a legacy. It's everyone's quest. It's in us to want to impress those around us. It's in us to want to leave our mark on the world.

Turned inwardly, that drive to impress others is dangerous. It is unquenchable, maybe even uncontrollable. It is easily usurped by that big ego we talked about in chapter 1—that skewed sense of self-importance we all possess in different doses. It pushes you to always want more—more stuff, more money, more position, more power, more fame. It's why Alexander the Great conquered the known world and cried because there were no more worlds to conquer. It's why Julius Caesar conquered the world two centuries later and cried at the monument of Alexander because Alexander did it all first and younger. At least the more recent world conqueror, Napoleon, was more honest. He accepted that glory is truly short-lived, but it was better than having no glory at all, because "obscurity lasts forever."

But turned outwardly toward others, legacy building can honor God. This type of drive in the pursuit of a godly legacy is not fleeting but lasting—everlasting. The reason is that it invests in people. Godly influence over another life is the legacy you want to leave behind, whether it be in obscurity or not.

This is what John Geddie did. John was a nineteenth-century Scottish-Canadian missionary to the Pacific islands known as New Hebrides (now Vanuatu). He's an inspiring example of living for Christ in a manner that left a godly legacy in his wake. Despite many setbacks and the loss of two little children, he sailed with his family to the other side of the world to tell of the love of Jesus Christ. It's hard for us to imagine the sacrifice this took. He not only exposed himself to unimaginable dangers in a new land with different climates, foreign languages, and strange illnesses, but he exposed his surviving loved ones too!

Most dangerous of all were the hostile islanders. They were known for eating humans, killing children, and sacrificing (by strangulation) recently widowed women—all as part of worship. Yet these were people loved by God. After several decades of ministry, John died. A memorial tablet was placed behind the pulpit in a little church he built on one of the islands. The inscription says it all:

In memory of John Geddie, D.D., born in Scotland, 1815, minister in Prince Edward Island seven years, Missionary sent from Nova Scotia to Aneiteum for twenty-four years. *When he landed in 1848, there were no Christians here, and when he left in 1872 there were no heathen.*[3]

Now, that's the godly legacy of a life lived for Jesus Christ!

THE BARNABAS WAY

God's view of legacy building is eternal in perspective. Getting highways and buildings named after you or making it on that rich list is not high on His list of lasting legacies. God gives no reward for ending life with the most money in your account!

Godly legacy is all about people. People are the only fruit of your labors on earth that will show up in eternity. Barnabas knew that fact and lived in light of it. Barnabas was farsighted. As a result, he aligned his life to that goal. In doing so, he followed Christ's pattern as expressed in His greatest commandment—love God through a love for people.[4] It is because Barnabas was farsighted that he was also a constant Christ follower. Living with eternity in mind developed from daily exposure to God.

And so we arrive at our last two principles that everyday Christians can adopt to shape their part of the world for Him. To detect them, we need to revisit some of the biblical passages we've already studied concerning Barnabas.

The Barnabas Way Focuses on a Godly Legacy

We left Barnabas sailing off to Cyprus with his arm around John Mark in Acts 15. We never hear of Barnabas again. He's gone. And that's OK. Barnabas wasn't building a name for himself, a place in history, a personal empire. We've seen that all along. I'm sure he will be quite shocked when many of us introduce ourselves to him as though we know him when we arrive at the new heaven and new earth. But look at the godly legacy Barnabas left for generations to come as he sailed off into obscurity.

Barnabas left us the apostle Paul. That's right! Barnabas's legacy is a person—the great apostle Paul. I've been leading here all along. When we think of Paul, we see him through the lens of the impact he had on Christianity for two thousand years. We see him as a giant of the faith. But in his own day, few saw that. He was abandoned by many within the Christian faith and martyred pretty much alone. But Barnabas saw what Paul could become for Christ from the start. And he was right. So Barnabas set his life on producing that.

. . . .

BARNABAS PRINCIPLE #14: *LEGACY*

A godly influencer views legacy not as *what's* left but *who's* left.

. . . .

Paul is arguably the greatest Christian theologian, author, evangelist, missionary, and martyr outside of Jesus Christ. God didn't use any other person the way He used Paul to write massive portions of the Scriptures. And many of his writings are not just letters—they are letters that help us understand the entire Old Testament Scriptures; they help us grasp history in light of the death, burial, and resurrection of Jesus Christ. These are theologically rich and indispensable contributions. God could have used someone else to launch Paul, but Barnabas was available to be God's choice. Barnabas invested himself in Paul. Barnabas gave us the apostle Paul.

Barnabas left us John Mark. Barnabas's legacy is also John Mark. Mark wrote one of the four gospels in the New Testament. It is a gospel that focuses on Jesus Christ as a faithful servant who calls His followers to faithful service. This is no coincidence. Mark knew all about failed service and of opportunities to pick oneself up under the right watchful eye. It is also likely that Mark's gospel is written under the influence of Peter, that other servant with a failed track record—three denials of Christ! Mark went on to minister alongside Peter as his assistant.

And not only did Mark write some of our Bible, like Paul, but many believe his gospel was consulted by Matthew and Luke when they wrote their gospels. And Luke wrote the book of Acts as well. The ripple effect is huge. My point is that this John Mark played a massive role in getting us the New Testament Scriptures.

Perhaps one of the most beautiful twists in church history are Paul's words in 2 Timothy 4:11. It's his last letter. He knew he would soon be martyred. He listed those who abandoned him. He asked Timothy for a coat to keep him warm and some books to read. And then he declared, "Get Mark and bring him with you, because he is helpful to me in my ministry." Mark became the great man Barnabas saw he could be. And Paul eventually got to see that too!

Godly influencers who finish well leave a trail of blessed people behind them. They fixate their lives on pouring themselves into others, not on getting more and more stuff. The results speak for themselves.

I love the ancient story of Pygmalion because it uses

ridicule to warn you about what you fixate your life on. Even ancient pagans knew of this human danger. In Ovid's poem *Metamorphoses*, we are introduced to Pygmalion: a king and sculptor. This king loved his work so much he devoted his life to it. One of his creations was the sculpture of a woman he carved out of ivory. It was a beautiful creation; it was his life's work. He fixated on her so long that he fell in love. Yes, he fell head over heels in love with the statue! It gets worse. He loved her so much, he married her.

Barnabas fixated on that most precious creation in God's eyes: people. He aligned his life to invest in people, love people, encourage people, launch people. Godly influencers do that. They view legacy not as *what's* left behind but *who's* left. It's all about godly influence on people. That changes a culture.

The Barnabas Way Is Content to Follow

God's influencers in culture are constant followers first. I like what British prime minister Benjamin Disraeli once said: "I must follow the people. Am I not their leader?" He was right. It's not just about learning to follow first so that one can lead later. It's about an ongoing posture of following so that one knows how to lead now. To lead is to follow first. That is not another contradiction. To lead is to follow God.

> **BARNABAS PRINCIPLE #15:**
> ***FOLLOW***
>
> A godly influencer is a constant God follower.

161

A follower of Jesus *follows* Jesus. This may be obvious, but it isn't simple. There are a lot of people wanting Jesus to keep up with their plans. But being a godly influencer is keeping up with Him. It is a life of self-denial; it is a walk in which we pick up our cross daily and follow Him (Luke 9:23). That's not simple. You can influence others well only *if* you are following God well yourself.

Barnabas copied God. It's back to that age-old *imitatio* we talked about. Barnabas was able to be a role model because God was his pattern. He followed God's lead; he was an imitator of God. To show you this in his life, we need to go back into the early passages in Acts where he was introduced: to the cameo appearance in Acts 9:27 (see chapter 3) and to the place we met him first in Acts 4:36 (see chapter 2).

If you recall, Acts 9 recounts a famous incident in Christian history—the conversion of the apostle Paul. The following should nudge your memory:

- The conversion and call of Paul (9:1–19a)
- The acceptance and rejection of Paul in Damascus (9:19b–25)
- The acceptance and rejection of Paul in Jerusalem (9:26–30)

We saw that Barnabas played a hinge role that opened up the doorway of Paul's acceptance into fellowship in the Christian church. And we saw that Barnabas was also the bridge Paul walked across into official Christian ministry. We said that the third section (9:26–30) unfolded with Paul trying to meet the Jerusalem church (9:26a), but he was rejected due to understandable suspicion and fear (9:26b). Yet, because Barnabas spoke up for him (9:27), Paul was able to join the Jerusalem church, including ministering so boldly in Jerusalem that he had to flee to Tarsus to evade a murder plot (9:28–30).

This exact same sequence of events happened already in Acts 9, just in a different city, Damascus (9:10–25). The author of Acts used an ancient device in storytelling called *syncrisis*. He presented two scenes in the exact same framing so that you connect the dots. It's like a literary version of the "match the objects" game that young kids do in educational books. Or like synchronized swimming at the Olympics—pool gymnasts dancing the exact same routine with every move perfectly matched by each swimmer. It's designed to catch your attention. You are supposed to connect the dots. The following table tries to connect the dots for you and make the point.

JERUSALEM (Acts 9:26–30)	DAMASCUS (Acts 9:10–25)
1. Disciples to meet Paul (26a)	1. Ananias to meet Paul (10–12)
2. Fear (26b)	2. Fear (13–14)
3. Barnabas intervenes (27)	3. God intervenes (15–19a)
4. Results (28–30): • Joins • Proclaims • Murder plot • Assisted escape	4. Results (19b–25): • Joins • Proclaims • Murder plot • Assisted escape

That means Barnabas was in sync with God when he spoke up for Paul; when you connect the dots, you see that Barnabas matched God. All that he did for Paul in Jerusalem was what God did for Paul in Damascus. That one verse featuring Barnabas is precisely the act that matches God's actions for Paul. That's quite the cameo appearance. Barnabas was in sync with God and followed His lead.

But this shouldn't surprise us. We've seen Barnabas copying God this entire time. His very nickname was the giveaway: "Joseph, a Levite from Cyprus, whom the apostles called Barnabas (which means 'son of encouragement')" (Acts 4:36). The author of Acts intentionally drew this out from the beginning when we met Barnabas for the first time. The nickname the apostles gave Barnabas means "son of encouragement," which literally means "son of Paraclesis." And that is precisely the nickname Jesus gives the Holy Spirit—the Encourager, the Comforter, the Paraclete (John 14:16, 26).

In the book of the acts of the Encourager (the acts of the Holy Spirit through the apostles), we have an individual who influenced others in such synchronization with God that he was given a new name to capture this characteristic: "Let's call him Barnabas, the son of the Paraclete," the apostles declared. For these men who coined the nickname, Barnabas was like the presence of the Holy Spirit in their midst.

All that to say, Barnabas copied God, following His pattern. Authentic, everyday Christians are constant God followers.

THE BARNABAS WAY THROUGH YOU

Legacy is not about making a name for yourself—that's shortsighted. In Jesus' kingdom, it's quite the opposite. Those who are genuine followers are farsighted; they live with an eternal perspective: an eternal intelligence. They heed Jesus' words that you influence from a posture of servanthood. That's Christ's pattern. That's living with an eternal perspective.

In Matthew 26, we see that Jesus' closest followers— the Twelve—struggled with legacy building. On the heels of Jesus telling them about His upcoming death, burial, and resurrection, two of them, the brothers James and John, sent their mom to ask for top positions of greatness in God's kingdom. The other ten, of course, got mad at them for doing this—but only because they also wanted the top spots. It's easy to pick on them now. The flaws of others seem so obvious to us. I'm sure if I were there back then, I'd be jostling for position too.

But Jesus' response rejects the world's definition of greatness: power, authority, and position. He is emphatic with His followers: Not so with you! That's what He told James, John, and the other ten, and it's His message to all who follow after Him: Not so with you! For Jesus, legacy means the opposite. The first is last. The greatest are the servants. That is God's way; that is the pattern Christ left. It is why He took a towel, got on His knees, and became a foot washer as one of His final lessons to the Twelve. He really did not come to be served but to serve.[5] There is no big-shot, power-crazy, climb-the-ladder-to-the-top approach in what Jesus modeled. That's why He declared emphatically, "Not so with you!"

Some Food for Thought

REMEMBER, YOU WILL BENEFIT MOST FROM ANSWER-
ing the following questions after reflecting on the key
sections in this chapter.

1. What legacy have you always wanted to leave behind?
   Be honest. Think about how the culture defines a worthwhile legacy.
2. Read Jesus' teaching on the Greatest Commandment
   and His act of washing the disciples' feet (Matthew
   22:37–40; Mark 12:29–31; John 13:1–17). Reflect on how
   these define and model a godly legacy.
3. Take a few moments to reflect on the impact of the
   apostle Paul and Mark on the Christian church. Barnabas
   stood behind them both. Then think about what God
   could do in those people around you if you launched
   them. How would you develop an eternal intelligence?

Conclusion

*Well done, good and faithful servant . . . Come
and share your master's happiness.*

JESUS

*The Lord helps us grow downward when we are
only thinking about growing upward.*

CHARLES H. SPURGEON

A FEW MONTHS INTO MY RETURN TO TEXAS TO TEACH at Dallas Theological Seminary, I found myself on hold on the phone with a home warranty insurance company. I didn't really know what a home warranty was since the service doesn't exist back where I am from. And to be honest, my wife always dealt with these house details. But she'd called them several times about fixing something in our new home and was frustrated at getting nowhere with them. So now it was my turn to get frustrated on the phone—for an hour.

Eventually, I got through to a representative and explained the situation. He instructed me to pick a tradesman from their list of several hundred in the Dallas–Fort Worth area. The list was just company names, so I had no idea who to pick. In light of that, I asked the representative to choose someone for me, assuming his guess was better than mine. He somewhat jokingly said he would run his finger down the list and stop randomly at one. After all, he wasn't in my area either. Each company on the list was as good as the next from both our perspectives.

A week later, someone from the company chosen at random called me. The man on the other end of the phone apologized profusely at the delay, explaining that he was the company owner and never does these calls. In fact, he was off on a family bereavement but noticed the call hadn't been made by an employee and just thought he'd do it himself. Now, his accent was a little tough to understand because he was from India. And no surprise, my Northern Irish accent was difficult for him too. So we had a bit of a laugh at the thought of an Indian man fixing a problem for a Northern Irishman in Texas.

Our conversation moved away from the broken item in our home to a mutual curiosity. We each wondered what the other was doing in the United States. I told him I was a preacher and professor at Dallas Seminary from Northern Ireland. He then told me he'd been to Northern Ireland many years before. As the conversation flowed, he also picked up that I'd grown up in the Canary Islands, Spain. And this made him all the more curious because he'd also visited the Canary Islands years before. This, of course, got me curious. Why had an Indian man in the United States traveled specifically to both these small places? Both the Canary Islands and Northern Ireland are not on the top-ten must-go places to visit.

As it turned out, he'd been on the ship of a ministry called Operation Mobilization that traveled the world sharing the gospel. And this made me laugh out loud because as a little boy I loved it when those ships occasionally came to the islands to minister alongside the few local churches there. It was a standout memory in my life.

And then the proverbial light bulb switched on. He said, "Wait a minute. When I was in the Canary Islands in the early eighties, I stayed with the family of one of the most remarkable men I've ever met. He had a wife and a few little boys. I've never forgotten him. In fact, it was his ministry to me those few weeks in his home that resulted in my marriage to my wife and my moving here to Texas. He, too, was from Northern Ireland. His name was Dennis Murphy. Do you know him?"

I couldn't believe what I was hearing.

"Do I know him?" I said, "I sure do. I'm one of those little boys you mentioned. I'm his son."

I had to pull the phone away from my ear, such was the shriek of amazement on the other side.

Remarkable! Here was a randomly picked Indian tradesman talking to a Northern Irishman living in Texas. Neither of us was supposed to be on the phone that day. Well, so it seemed. God, of course, was the one having a little fun. Though many issues stand out about this conversation—God's providential fun being one—the point was my dad's influence on this Indian man more than thirty years before. It was a godly influence he never forgot.

Dad shaped his life!

VENI. VIDI. SERVI.

People shape people. It's a basic reality I've been hammering on about this entire time. Remember, we're made of clay, and every one of us is molded by exposure to others. We rub off on one another for good or ill.

This book has argued that Jesus' call in the Great Commission works with this basic truth. Every follower *of*

Jesus is to influence those around them *for* Jesus. Title, position, age, expertise, mood, qualifications, and so on don't determine whether you do this. No exceptions. There's no subcontracting this out to your pastor. Sitting in the bleachers as a spectator is not allowed. Every follower is to be a godly influencer. Every follower is to be a servant leader to some extent. Every follower must go and make disciples! This really matters. And this really can occur in a most natural and doable way in your daily comings and goings in life. It really doesn't matter what your station in life is. God has a knack for using everyday Christians to accomplish His extraordinary dream of reshaping the world.

God even gives us a role model to copy: Barnabas. By now you know this! This role model stands in sharp contrast to the ones we tend to parade when following the world's view on influence and leadership.

Remember the Roman leader Julius Caesar? He's that world conqueror who cried with jealousy at the statue of Alexander the Great. His motto in life was "Veni. Vidi. Vici." ("I came. I saw. I conquered.") It drips with selfish ambition, self-importance, and a self-proclamation of his own greatness. It's a call to climb, grab, reach some summit, and make a name for yourself. Get! Conquer! To be fair, Caesar did leave his stamp on the world. He even got a month in our calendar named after him: July. But it's not a time marker in heaven.

Barnabas stands in stark contrast to the likes of Julius Caesar. If Barnabas (and Latin grammarians) will forgive me, I would say his life displayed more of the motto "Veni. Vidi.

Servi." ("I came. I saw. I served.")[1] No world conquered. No ladder climbed to the top. No month named after him. Barnabas just sailed into the sunset toward Cyprus and off the pages of known history with his arm around a discouraged young believer. We never hear of him again. But he is God's hand-picked role model for you to copy. God puts him in the Bible for us.

Barnabas is that practical and accessible God-given pattern for us as we go out to be salty influencers and bright bulbs for Jesus. He embodies the fifteen basic principles that any ordinary believer can adapt, customize, and embody. He's there to be copied. It doesn't matter whether you are a mom, dad, student, teacher, CEO, salesperson, manager, doctor, gardener, builder, banker, pastor, lawyer, or retiree. You get the point! If you are a follower *of* Jesus, start by customizing these principles *for* Jesus with whoever happens to be nearby. Here you have them in one spot:

1. **INFLUENCE**: A godly influencer saturates any and every environment for God.
2. **VISION**: A godly influencer sees through God's eyes.
3. **ACTION**: A godly influencer serves as God's hands given God's heart.
4. **DISCERNMENT**: A godly influencer detects potential in others.
5. **RISK:** A godly influencer takes risks, and people are always risky!
6. **LEAD**: A godly influencer leads.

7. **DELEGATE**: A godly influencer delegates but doesn't compete.

8. **EMPOWER**: A godly influencer launches potential in protégés.

9. **EXAMPLE**: A godly influencer develops by example—hands-on!

10. **TRUTH**: A godly influencer is resolute for the absolute.

11. **CHANGE**: A godly influencer manages change well.

12. **CONFLICT**: A godly influencer handles tension well.

13. **OPPORTUNITY**: A godly influencer never wastes a mistake; instead, they recycle failures.

14. **LEGACY**: A godly influencer views legacy not as *what's* left but *who's* left.

15. **FOLLOW**: A godly influencer is a constant God follower.

Jesus' parting words—the Great Commission—are that His followers would go and make disciples. The welcoming words you will want to hear as you stand before Him one day are "Well done, good and faithful servant . . . Come and share in your master's happiness" (Matthew 25:23). And you will! Through faith in Jesus, you can live responsibly for Jesus. If each of us forms godly influencers as Barnabas did, and if the church gets godly, servant leadership as a result, then perhaps Christianity will spread again at unprecedented growth rates across the world and reclaim our culture for Jesus Christ!

ME HIDE. ME WIN. YOUR TURN!

Allow me to close with a story as a call for you to step up to influence for Christ. I have four kids, and they can be lots of fun. Like most kids, they love to play games. My youngest son is particularly keen on a combination of foot racing and hide-and-seek these days. He'll come up to me at home and shout, "Let's run!" and then take off toward some self-designated finish line, assuming I'm racing too, and always stare at his own feet as if impressed by their speed. After a few moments, he'll stop and shout back at me, "Me run. Me win." It's his victory taunt. He won!

This often leads to a game of hide-and-seek. He'll say, "Me hide, Dad," and off he goes as I count out loud to ten. It's fun pretending not to see him hiding behind his hands as they cover his eyes. And when I finally *don't* find him (to save tears of ending the game too soon), his victory taunt is "Me hide. Me win. Your turn!" Then off I go as he counts. It's brilliant fun.

Then one day my wife and I, along with my youngest, James, were in a huge furniture store. It was massive. I'd never been in one this big: Texas big! James, presumably a little bored, turned to me and shouted, "Let's run!" and took off, with me in hot pursuit. It wasn't long before he stopped and, of course, proclaimed victory: "Me run. Me win." This worked out quite well because he ran to the area of the store we were wanting to stop at: armchairs.

After a little while perusing the selection, my wife and I looked at each other and simultaneously said, "Where's James?" James was nowhere to be seen. He was gone and who knows for how long!

Panic kicked in. My wife and I took off in different directions, calling out to him. There was no response. As time unfolded we got louder and louder and even more desperate. Child abductions happen, and this place was huge and with multiple exits. It became clear to everyone nearby there was a problem. A manager passing by made the call to announce through the store speakers, "Code Adam. Code Adam." At that point, the entire store went into lockdown. For fifteen minutes the store was shut as staff policed the exit doors and looked for James. It was every parent's nightmare. Pure fear and worry ran through my veins as I prayed, "Am I ever going to see him again, Lord? I'll do anything to have him back. Please, Lord, give me back my son. I just want to hug him and hear his voice again." It was horrible!

And then, in the distance, I saw this huge man wearing a store uniform smiling from ear to ear and walking toward me. He is now my image of an angel because holding his hand was my little James. I ran toward him wiping away tears, and as I got close I saw him look to the man while pointing at me, and say, "Dat's my dadda." I lifted him into my arms and toward my teary face and got to hear that little voice again.

And what were those glorious first words? That's right, the victory taunt: "Me hide. Me win. Your turn!"

Hide-and-seek. It's fun in certain contexts but not in

others. Yes at home. No in huge furniture stores. It's banned for an indefinite period of time in the Murphy family. And while it is a fun and harmless game for kids, it got me thinking about another place hide-and-seek is often played and must stop: the Christian life and the Great Commission. If you are a follower of Jesus Christ, the Great Commission makes it clear that hide-and-seek is not a legitimate game to play. In our call to influence the world for Jesus Christ, "Me hide" is "Me *no* win!"

No more hiding. God has a knack for using everyday believers like you and me to shape His world for Christ. Remember, it is our turn now—flaws and all!

PS. Oh! One final story. Last summer I visited my brother who pastors a church in Spain. My dad was also there for the week. One morning, very early, as I made my way to the kitchen for breakfast, I noticed the door partly open in my brother's study. I peeked in to see if he was there. And what scene did I behold? That beautiful childhood picture—now refreshed before me again—of Dad on his knees with face in hands in prayer, meeting

with our great God. The prayers that molded my life were still rising to God for Him to do a work, now in his granddaughters and grandsons. Thanks to smartphones, I got a great photo. That memory will now never fade. The impact lives on!

Some Food for Thought

HERE ARE SOME FINAL QUESTIONS TO CONSIDER. Remember to answer them after reflecting on the main ideas of this chapter.

1. Jesus entrusted the Great Commission to Christians in Matthew 28:19–20. What stands in your way of getting directly involved in its fulfillment?

2. Look back over our list of fifteen principles of godly influence. As you reflect on them, think about a person in your day-to-day life you could come alongside. What is a doable plan of action for you to begin implementing these principles to influence this person?

3. In the parable of the talents in Matthew 25:14–30, Jesus taught His followers concerning spiritual service. It is here where we read those words we all desire to one day hear: "Well done, good and faithful servant." Read this parable with an eye on Jesus' teaching on faithful and unfaithful stewardship. What people has He entrusted to you?

Acknowledgments

THIS BOOK WAS TRULY A GROUP EFFORT. I'VE SIMPLY had the joy of putting to paper what others taught me and modelled for me over several decades.

And so, a special thank you goes to several groups of people.

Thank you to the outstanding team at the W Publishing Group—especially to Damon Reiss and Kyle Olund for believing in the importance of the message of this work for today, and also to the rest of the team for working tirelessly to put it in your hands.

Thank you, Drs. Elliott Johnson, Stanley Toussaint, and "Prof" Hendricks for introducing me to Barnabas back in 2003–2004. They repeatedly encouraged me to write about him all those years ago and so I did (finally!).

Thank you, Pastor Chuck Swindoll and Mr. Sealy Yates. Without your encouragement, Chuck, and your practical help and wisdom, Sealy, this book would not exist. You've been dear friends and mentors to me.

Thank you, Mom and Dad! Mom, you taught me the

Scriptures as far back as my memory goes, and Dad, you modelled for me the *Barnabas-like* life. Thank you for loving Jesus the way you've both done for your many children and many, many more grandchildren.

And a very special thank you to my wife, Sarah Jane, for your constant love and support, and to my children, Sienna, Joshua, Jake, and James, for your patience with a busy dad. I love each of you dearly.

As I said, a group effort. Thank you all!

Notes

Introduction

1. "The Economic Impact of the Coffee Industry," National Coffee Association USA, accessed January 17, 2020, http://www.ncausa.org/industry-resources/economic-impact.
2. Genesis 2:7; 3:19.
3. Alan Kreider, "They Alone Know the Right Way to Live," in *Ancient Faith for the Church's Future*, eds. Mark Husbands and Jeffrey P. Greenman (Downers Grove, IL: InterVarsity Press, 2008), 169. See also E. Glenn Hinson, *The Evangelization of the Roman Empire: Identity and Adaptability* (Macon, GA: Mercer University Press, 1981), 49–50.
4. Romans 14:10–12; 2 Corinthians 5:10.
5. Philippians 2:11.
6. Gene A. Getz, *The Apostles: Becoming Unified Through Diversity* (Nashville, TN: Broadman & Holman, 1998), 3–4.

Chapter 1

1. Andrew A. Woolsey, *Channel of Revival: A Biography of Duncan Campbell* (Edinburgh: The Faith Mission, 1974), 22.
2. Andrew James Symington, "John Campbell, the Ledaig Poet, at Home," *The Celtic Magazine* 13, no. 154 (August 1888): 473–80; Andrew James Symington, "John Campbell, of Ledaig: The Gaelic Bard and His Home," *The Celtic Monthly: A Magazine for Highlanders* 1, no. 4 (January 1893): 58.

3. Warren Bennis, *Managing People Is Like Herding Cats: Warren Bennis on Leadership* (Provo, UT: Executive Excellence Publishing, 1999), 163.
4. Exodus 3–4.
5. James M. Kouzes and Barry Z. Posner, *The Leadership Challenge: How to Make Extraordinary Things Happen in Organizations*, 6th ed. (Hoboken, NJ: John Wiley & Sons, 2007), 25.
6. George Barna, "Nothing Is More Important Than Leadership," in *Leaders on Leadership: Wisdom, Advice, and Encouragement on the Art of Leading God's People*, ed. George Barna (Ventura, CA: Regal Books, 1997), 18. See also "Christians on Leadership, Calling, and Career," Barna, June 3, 2013, https://www.barna.com/research/christians-on-leadership-calling-and-career/#; and "82% of Young Adults Say Society Is in a Leadership Crisis," adapted from Barna and World Vision's worldwide survey and report, *The Connected Generation*, 2019, Barna, October 30, 2019, https://www.barna.com/research/leadership-crisis/.
7. Seneca, *Epistles: On Sharing Knowledge* 6.5–7.
8. Cicero, *De Oratore* 2.22.
9. Kouzes and Posner, *Leadership Challenge*, 297.

Chapter 2

1. The World War II hero topped a nationwide poll of the one hundred greatest Britons in history. "Churchill Voted Greatest Briton," BBC News, November 24, 2002, http://news.bbc.co.uk/2/hi/entertainment/2509465.stm.
2. Robert Greenleaf, *The Servant as Leader*, rev. ed., (South Orange, NJ: Greenleaf Center for Servant Leadership, 2015), 7.
3. Warren Bennis, quoted in Dianna Booher, *Executive's Portfolio of Model Speeches for All Occasions* (Englewood Cliffs, New Jersey: Prentice Hall Direct, 1991), 34.

4. Daniel Gilbert, *Stumbling on Happiness* (New York: Knopf, 2006): 5–6.

5. H. A. Ironside, *In the Heavenlies: Practical Expository Addresses on the Epistle to the Ephesians* (New York: Loizeaux Brothers, 1937), 51–58.

6. Gyles Brandreth, *The Joy of Lex: How to Have Fun with 860,341,500 Words* (New York: Morrow, 1980).

7. It is impossible to find where Saint-Exupéry said this exact phrase despite its common citation. It is certainly a close cousin to what he writes elsewhere on this theme. See "Citadelle," in *Oeuvres* (Paris: Gallimard, 1959), 687.

8. Steven Sloman and Philip Fernbach, *The Knowledge Illusion: Why We Never Think Alone* (New York: Riverhead Books, 2017); Daniel Goleman, *Emotional Intelligence: Why It Matters More Than IQ* (New York: Bantam Books, 1995).

Chapter 3

1. Thomas Cahill, *How the Irish Saved Civilization: The Untold Story of Ireland's Heroic Role from the Fall of Rome to the Rise of Medieval Europe* (New York: Anchor Books, 1995).

2. David Baker, "Mickey, the East End Hero," *Optician*, February 1, 2013, 11–12. See also Dan Cruickshank, *Spitalfields: The History of a Nation in a Handful of Streets* (London: Random House Books, 2016), 585–608; Richie Calder, *Carry On London!* (London: English Universities Press, 1941); and Mike Brooke, "Mickey Davis at the Fruit & Wool Exchange," March 6, 2012, Spitalfields Life, https://spitalfieldslife.com/2012/03/06/mickey-davis-at-the-fruit-wool-exchange/.

3. See the work of Howard Gardner, *Multiple Intelligences: New Horizons* (New York: Basic Books, 2006).

Chapter 4

1. This is according to a survey in 1987. See "Rolls-Royce Shares Will Fly," *The Times*, April 29, 1987.

2. Max De Pree, *Leadership Is an Art* (New York: Dell Publishing, 1989), 59, emphasis added.

3. 1 Corinthians 12:12–26; Ephesians 2:21–22.

4. Josephus, *Jewish Wars* 3.29.

5. De Pree, *Leadership Is an Art*, 9.

6. Kouzes and Posner, *Leadership Challenge*, 131–32; V. Lieberman, S. M. Samuels, and L. Ross, "The Name of the Game: Predictive Power of Reputations Versus Situational Labels in Determining Prisoner's Dilemma Game Moves," *Personality and Social Psychology Bulletin* 30, no. 9 (2004): 1175–85.

Chapter 5

1. Vishal Mangalwadi, *The Legacy of William Carey: A Model for the Transformation of a Culture* (Wheaton: Crossway, 1999), 24.

2. Eustace Carey, *Memoir of William Carey, D.D.*, (London: Jackson and Walford, 1836), quoted in Abraham Kuruvilla, *A Manual for Preaching: The Journey from Text to Sermon* (Grand Rapids: Baker Academic, 2019), 199.

3. Joseph Laconte, *A Hobbit, A Wardrobe, and a Great War: How J. R. R. Tolkien and C. S. Lewis Rediscovered Faith, Friendship, and Heroism in the Cataclysm of 1914–1918* (Nashville, TN: Nelson Books, 2015), xvii; Humphrey Carpenter, *J. R. R. Tolkien: A Biography* (Boston: Houghton Mifflin, 1987), 89.

4. Humphrey Carpenter, ed., *The Letters of J. R. R. Tolkien* (Boston: Houghton Mifflin, 2000), 88.

5. Crerar Douglas, ed., *Autobiography of Augustus Hopkins Strong* (Valley Forge, PA: Judson Press, 1981), 300.

6. Charles Spurgeon, "9 Ways to Pray like Charles Spurgeon," The Spurgeon Center, October 27, 2016, https://www.spurgeon.org

/resource-library/blog-entries/9-ways-to-pray-like-charles
-spurgeon/.

7. Justo L. Gonzalez, *The Story of Christianity*, vol. 2, *The Reformation to the Present Day* (New York: Harper, 1985), 306.

Chapter 6

1. Thomas Cahill, *Heretics and Heroes: How Renaissance Artists and Reformation Priests Created Our World* (New York: Anchor Books, 2013), 177.

2. Heiko A. Oberman, *Luther: Man Between God and the Devil* (New York: Image Books, 1992), 197.

3. Oberman, *Luther*, 198.

4. Forell and Lehman, *Luther's Works*, 32:113.

5. "Word of the Year 2016," Oxford Languages, accessed September 16, 2019, https://languages.oup.com /word-of-the-year/word-of-the-year-2016.

6. John S. Dickerson, *Hope of Nations: Standing Strong in a Post-Truth, Post-Christian World* (Grand Rapids: Zondervan, 2018), 80.

7. Alexander Solzhenitsyn's Nobel Prize lecture is available at https://www.nobelprize.org/prizes/literature/1970 /solzhenitsyn/lecture/.

8. Thomas J. Heffernan, *The Passion of Perpetua and Felicity* (New York: Oxford University Press, 2012).

9. Martin Orridge, *Change Leadership: Developing a Change-Adept Organization* (Surrey, UK: Gower Publishing, 2009), xiii. He also humorously and accurately notes, "In today's business world it is not the Grim Reaper, but Change who sits constantly at our shoulder. It could be said that the Grim Reaper generally only appears if we have failed to heed the voice of Change" (xiii).

10. Bob Smietana, "Lifeway Research: Americans Are Fond of the Bible, Don't Actually Read It," Lifeway Research, April 25, 2017, https://lifewayresearch.com/2017/04/25/lifeway-research -americans-are-fond-of-the-bible-dont-actually-read-it/.

Chapter 7

1. Dan B. Allender, *Leading with a Limp: Take Full Advantage of Your Most Powerful Weakness* (Colorado Springs, CO: WaterBrook Press, 2006), 2.
2. Samuel R. Chand, *Leadership Pain: The Classroom for Growth* (Nashville, TN: Nelson Books, 2015), 35.
3. Chand, *Leadership Pain*, 35.
4. J. Robert Clinton, *The Making of a Leader* (Colorado Springs, CO: NavPress, 2006), 53.
5. Chand, *Leadership Pain*, 14, quoting Philip Yancey, *Reaching for the Invisible God* (Grand Rapids: Zondervan, 2000), 69.
6. De Pree, *Leadership Is an Art*, 59.
7. Cahill, *How the Irish Saved Civilization*, 199–204.
8. Cahill, *Heretics and Heroes*, 110–11.
9. De Pree, *Leadership Is an Art*, 11.

Chapter 8

1. Roy Jenkins, *Churchill: A Biography* (New York: Farrar, Straus, and Giroux, 2001), 825. The essay is also available for reading online. See "'The Dream': A Fictional Encounter by Winston S. Churchill," The Churchill Project, April 2, 2018, https://winstonchurchill.hillsdale.edu/winston-churchills-dream-1947/.
2. Jenkins, *Churchill*, 825. See also Boris Johnson, *The Churchill Factor: How One Man Made History* (London: Hodder & Stoughton, 2014), 45.
3. E. Myers Harrison, *Blazing the Missionary Trail* (Wheaton: Van Kampen Press, 1949), 58.
4. Matthew 22:37–40; Mark 12:29–31.
5. John 13; Matthew 20:20–28.

Conclusion

1. I know, it is *serve* in Latin, not *servi*. But you must admit, for my purposes here *servi* has a better ring to it. Forgive me!

About the Author

S. JONATHAN MURPHY IS A PROFESSOR, PASTOR, AND author. He is the Department Chair of Pastoral Ministries at Dallas Theological Seminary, a board member of Insight for Living Ministries, and a teaching pastor at Christ Chapel Bible Church in Fort Worth, TX. He also enjoys cheering for his children in sports from the sidelines and shouting at the TV when watching his beloved Ulster rugby team play. Jonathan's cross-cultural ministry is wide in scope. He was born in Northern Ireland, raised in Spain as a missionary kid, educated in Scotland, and Texas. He resides in Texas with his wife, Sarah Jane, and their four children.

www.sjonathanmurphy.com